Michael Harris • David Mo[...]

WORLD CLASS
LEVEL 3

STUDENTS' BOOK

LONGMAN

Summary of course content

Learning to learn

A Learning English
Students' Book
Reading	Skimming the book
Speaking	Questionnaire: study habits
	Discussion: contact with English
Speaking/Listening	Classroom language

Activity Book
Listening	Study habits and self-assessment
Reading	Using the book

B A star
Students' Book
Speaking	Survey: favourite stars
Reading	Magazine article: film star
Learner training	Reading strategies/Remembering words/Organising vocabulary books

Activity Book
Learner training	Using the mini-dictionary/Vocabulary books
Vocabulary revision	Hobbies and animals

C Your life
Students' Book
Learner training	Listening strategies/Editing a letter/Grammar: tenses game
Listening	Dialogues: routines
Speaking	Talking about routines

Activity Book
Learner training	Grammar: identifying tenses; organising grammar notes/Storing vocabulary
Writing	Informal letter

Module 1: Cities

1 Great cities
Students' Book
Speaking	City game
Reading	Travel brochure/Postcard
Writing	Writing a postcard
Learner training	Vocabulary from text/Phrasal verbs

Activity Book
Listening	Radio programme
Language revision	**Present perfect**

2 On tour
Students' Book
Listening	Radio interview
Language focus	**Present perfect: *still/yet/already* / Present perfect/Past simple**
	Travel game

Activity Book
Language focus	***Still/yet/already*, present perfect/ Past simple** / Travel questionnaire

3 Lifestyles
Students' Book
Listening	Conversation: leisure
Speaking	Leisure survey/Discussion: city or country?
Reading	City description
Writing	Describing a city

Activity Book
Reading	Description of character
Language revision	**Adverbs of frequency**
Vocabulary revision	Adjectives

4 Old and new
Students' Book
Language focus	**Comparative adjectives/**Writing descriptions/Guessing game
Pronunciation	Word stress

Activity Book
Reading	Amazing but true
Language focus	**Comparative adjectives**
Pronunciation	Word stress

5 Getting around
Students' Book
Learner training	Reading text types
Reading	Newspaper article
Speaking	Transport survey/Roleplay: tourist office
Listening	Dialogue: tourist office
Pronunciation	Intonation: polite requests

Activity Book
Reading	London guide
Language revision	**Prepositions of movement/**Directions
Vocabulary revision	Places and adjectives

6 Going out
Students' Book
Writing	Cities project: listing places
Listening	Conversation: weekend plans
Language focus	**Plans and intentions**

SUMMARY OF COURSE CONTENT

Activity Book
Language focus	Plans and intentions
Listening	Conversation: plans
Vocabulary revision	Hobbies/chores

7 Revision
Students' Book
Listening	City quiz
Speaking	Talking about plans/Leisure survey
Language revision	Comparatives/Present perfect/Intentions
Learner training	Using cognates/Grammar notes/Progress review

Activity Book
Language revision	Test yourself
Learner training	Storing vocabulary
Game	Crossword: cities

Module 2: Yesterday

8 Living in the past
Students' Book
Learner training	Vocabulary classification
Speaking	Talking about the past
Speaking/Reading	Reading jigsaw: Aztecs and Vikings

Activity Book
Listening	Ancient Chinese
Language revision	Past simple
Pronunciation	Past tense endings
Learner training	Vocabulary classification

9 History makers
Students' Book
Reading	Historical cartoon
Language focus	Past simple: irregular verbs/Quiz
Listening	Life story

Activity Book
Reading	Biography: Marco Polo
Vocabulary revision	Materials
Language focus	Past simple/*Could* / *Had to*

10 King Arthur
Students' Book
Listening	The Sword in the Stone
Writing	Linking words
Learner training	Word building
Pronunciation	/aɪ/ /ɪ/ /ɜː/

Activity Book
Reading	Cartoon story
Language revision	Past simple questions
Pronunciation	/aɪ/ /ɪ/ /ɜː/

11 Memories
Students' Book
Listening	Interview: memories
Language focus	Past habits: *used to*
Pronunciation	Decoding contractions

Activity Book
Language focus	Past habits: *used to*
Reading	Questionnaire: habits

12 Hard times
Students' Book
Reading	Reports from 1842
Speaking	Discussion: reactions
Speaking/Writing	Children's rights
Pronunciation	Silent letters

Activity Book
Reading	Oliver Twist
Language revision	Pronouns and possessive adjectives
Listening	Workhouse dialogue
Learner training	Phrasal verbs

13 Og
Students' Book
Learner training	Using encyclopedias
Reading	Imaginary encyclopedia extract
Language focus	Past simple/Present perfect/Grammar game

Activity Book
Language focus	Past simple/Present perfect/*For, since, ago*
Listening	Letter dictation
Game	Word search

14 Revision
Students' Book
Listening	History quiz
Speaking	Memories/experiences
Language revision	*Used to*/Past simple/Present perfect
Learner training	Phrasal verbs/Vocabulary questionnaire/Progress review
Writing	Biography

Activity Book
Language revision	Test yourself
Learner training	Storing vocabulary
Game	Word square

Module 3: Fantasy

15 World of horror
Students' Book
Listening	Interviews: fears
Pronunciation	Sentence stress
Speaking	Fear survey
Reading	Jumbled stories/Linking words

Activity Book
Pronunciation	Dictation
Language revision	Talking about fears
Vocabulary revision	Animals

16 The haunted house
Students' Book
Reading	Diary extract
Language focus	**Past simple/Past continuous**

Activity Book
Language focus	**Past simple/Past continuous**
Vocabulary revision	Rooms

17 Fantastic films
Students' Book
Speaking	Films/Making arrangements
Listening	Dialogue: arrangements
Pronunciation	Linking

Activity Book
Reading	The underground world (Episode 1)
Writing	Taking notes/Individual report
Language revision	**Suggestions**
Listening	Dialogue
Vocabulary revision	Types of films

18 The rescue
Students' Book
Reading	Story: The rescue
Language focus	**Past perfect**/Backward story game

Activity Book
Reading	Jumbled story
Language focus	**Past perfect**/Psychic questionnaire

19 Monsters
Students' Book
Reading	Monster descriptions
Learner training	Writing strategies
Writing	Describing monsters
Speaking	Describe and draw

Activity Book
Reading	The underground world (Episode 2)
Writing	Taking notes/Individual report
Listening	Werewolf description
Language revision	**Order of adjectives**
Writing	Describing a werewolf

20 Believe it or not?
Students' Book
Listening	Story: James Bartley
Reading	Newspaper article
Language focus	**Linking: past tenses**/Telling stories

Activity Book
Language focus	**Past tenses/Short answers**
Game	Word snake

21 Revision
Students' Book
Listening	Horror quiz
Speaking	Ghost reports
Language revision	**Past tenses**/Editing
Learner training	Grading mistakes/Progress review
Writing	Horror story

Activity Book
Reading	The underground world (Episode 3)
Writing	Taking notes/Individual report
Language revision	**Test yourself**
Learner training	Storing vocabulary
Game	Word jigsaw

Module 4: Nature

22 The seasons
Students' Book
Speaking	Nature questionnaire
Listening	Interview: the Mojave Desert
Pronunciation	/ɒ/ /ʌ/ /əʊ/ /ʊː/ /ɔː/
Writing	Nature project: describing a season

Activity Book
Reading	Lifecycle of squirrel
Language revision	**Question words**
Pronunciation	/ɒ/ /ʌ/ /əʊ/ /ʊː/ /ɔː/

23 Wonders of nature
Students' Book
Reading	Animal descriptions
Language focus	**Superlatives**/Animal quiz

SUMMARY OF COURSE CONTENT

Activity Book
Reading — Amazing but false
Listening — Guessing animals
Language focus — **Superlatives**
Learner training — Vocabulary classification
Writing — Nature project: animal description

24 Your planet needs you!
Students' Book
Reading — Green leaflet
Listening — Interview
Speaking — 'Green' survey
Writing — Nature project: help the planet

Activity Book
Reading — Rainforests
Language revision — **Present simple/Present continuous**
Learner training — Compound words

25 Takuana island
Students' Book
Learner training — Listening to English/Listening strategies
Listening — Radio programme
Language focus — **Conditional sentences (1)**
Pronunciation — Sentence stress: key words

Activity Book
Listening — Interview with scientist
Language focus — **Conditional sentences (1)**
Vocabulary revision — Places

26 Speak out!
Students' Book
Reading — Formal letter
Writing — Linking/Project: formal letter
Speaking — Simulation: debate

Activity Book
Listening — Class debate
Language revision — **Opinions**
Learner training — Connotations

27 Operation Tiger
Students' Book
Reading — Book extract
Language focus — **Relative clauses**/Guessing definitions/Project: writing definitions

Activity Book
Reading — Dolphins
Language focus — **Relative clauses**
Writing — Animal in danger
Vocabulary revision — Parts of animals

28 Revision
Students' Book
Listening — Nature watch project
Speaking — Predictions: animal guessing game
Language revision — **Relative pronouns**/Editing
Learner training — Mini-dictionary: sounds; phonetics/Progress review
Writing — Nature project: publicity production

Activity Book
Language revision — **Test yourself**
Learner training — Storing vocabulary
Reading — Jokes

Module 5: Sport

29 The world of sport
Students' Book
Learner training — Vocabulary classification
Speaking — Sports survey/Guessing game
Reading — Amazing but false

Activity Book
Listening — Unusual sport
Language revision — **Short answers**
Writing — Describing a sport

30 I hate sport!
Students' Book
Reading/Speaking — Sports questionnaire
Listening — Dialogue from questionnaire
Language focus — **Agreeing and disagreeing**
Pronunciation — Sentence stress

Activity Book
Language focus — **Agreeing and disagreeing**
Vocabulary revision — Clothes

31 Champions
Students' Book
Speaking — Survey: top sports people
Reading — Biography: Pelé
Learner training — Mini-dictionary game

Activity Book
Reading — Biography: Martina Navratilova
Language revision — **Prepositions of time**

32 Clubs
Students' Book
Listening — Dialogue: sports club
Language focus — **Question tags**/Question tag game
Pronunciation — Intonation: question tags

Activity Book
Language focus	Question tags
Vocabulary revision	Sports crossword

33 Warming up
Students' Book
Listening	Interview with P.E. expert
Writing	Giving advice: *because; to*/Instructions for exercise
Reading	Instructions

Activity Book
Language revision	**Giving advice**
Listening	Advice about swimming
Vocabulary	Parts of the body: shape poem

34 Armchair sport
Students' Book
Speaking	TV survey
Reading	Television guide
Listening	Sports commentaries
Language focus	**Adverbs**/Adverb game

Activity Book
Listening	Commentary: horse race
Reading	Questionnaire: speaking English
Language focus	**Adverbs**
Vocabulary revision	Television programmes

35 Revision
Students' Book
Listening	Sports quiz
Speaking	Checking information/Copy-cat game
Language revision	**Tense review/Questions/Adverbs**
Learner training	Speaking English/Self-assessment/Progress review
Writing	Describing a sport

Activity Book
Language revision	Test yourself
Learner training	Storing vocabulary
Board game	The road to gold

Module 6: Space

36 Our solar system
Students' Book
Reading	Magazine article
Speaking	Working out ages/Imaginary planet

Activity Book
Reading	The Dogon tribe
Language revision	**Questions with *how***

37 Science fact or fiction?
Students' Book
Speaking	Discussing the future
Listening	Interview with scientist
Language focus	**Talking about the future/Predictions**
Pronunciation	Word stress

Activity Book
Listening	Computer information
Language focus	**Future with *may/might/will***
Vocabulary revision	Planets: word grid

38 Your stars
Students' Book
Reading	Horoscopes
Writing	Linking/Horoscopes
Speaking	Discussing horoscopes

Activity Book
Listening	Horoscopes
Language revision	**Adjectives and prepositions**
Vocabulary revision	Adjectives
Pronunciation	Sounds dictation

39 A space colony
Students' Book
Reading	Description of colony
Language focus	**Present simple passive**

Activity Book
Language focus	**Passives**
Writing	Inventing a flag

40 Marathon men
Students' Book
Speaking	Discussion: living in space/Roleplay: interview
Reading	Magazine article
Listening	Interview
Writing	Diary notes
Pronunciation	Consonant clusters

Activity Book
Reading	Space food
Language revision	***Feel* + adjective**
Writing	Guided biography

41 Time travel
Students' Book
Speaking	Planning a time capsule
Listening	Dialogue: time travel
Language focus	**Conditional sentences (2)**
Pronunciation	/ɑː/ /æ/ /eɪ/ /e/ /ɔː/

SUMMARY OF COURSE CONTENT

Activity Book
Language focus	Conditionals
Vocabulary revision	Numbers and shapes

42 Revision
Students' Book
Listening	Dial-a-horoscope
Speaking	Prediction game/Strange situations
Language revision	*Passives*/Tense revision
Learner training	Word building/Progress review
Pronunciation	Study strategies/Difficult words
Writing	Science fiction story

Activity Book
Language revision	Test yourself
Learner training	Storing vocabulary: pronunciation
Game	Sound puzzle

Module 7: School

43 Lessons
Students' Book
Reading	Novel extract
Speaking	Lesson survey/Ideal lessons

Activity Book
Reading	Bonnie (Episode 1)
Language focus	*Like + gerund/infinitive*
Vocabulary revision	School subjects

44 Monk on the run
Students' Book
Reading	Magazine article
Language focus	*Some/any/no/every*, etc./Information gap: school roleplay/School project: complaints

Activity Book
Language focus	*Something/anything*, etc.
Vocabulary revision	Classroom objects

45 Excuses
Students' Book
Reading/Listening	Poem
Pronunciation	Intonation
Speaking	Information gap: excuses roleplay
Writing	School project: questionnaire

Activity Book
Reading	Bonnie (Episode 2)
Listening	Dialogue: excuses
Pronunciation	Marking intonation
Language revision	Questions with/without auxiliaries

46 Rules
Students' Book
Reading	School rules
Listening	Dialogue
Language focus	**Obligation and permission**/School project: ideal rules

Activity Book
Language focus	**Obligation and permission**
Writing	Party poster
Vocabulary revision	Word search: school subjects

47 Pupil profile
Students' Book
Reading	School report
Learner training	Grading mistakes/Assessing writing
Writing	School report/School project: report
Speaking	Discussing work

Activity Book
Reading	Bonnie (Episode 3)
Listening	Dialogue
Learner training	Self-assessment
Language revision	**Countables/uncountables**

48 Your school
Students' Book
Listening	Descriptions of schools
Language focus	**Expressions of location**/Information gap: school plans/School project: plan of ideal school
Pronunciation	/e/ /iː/ /ɪ/ /ə/

Activity Book
Language focus	**Expressions of location**
Vocabulary revision	Furniture
Pronunciation	/e/ /iː/ /ɪ/ /ə/

49 Revision
Students' Book
Listening	Excuses dialogues
Speaking	Advice about English/Describing your school
Language revision	*Anything/something*/**Obligation/Permission/Location**
Learner training	Word building/Sentence structure/End of year self-evaluation
Writing	School project: production

Activity Book
Language revision	Test yourself
Learner training	Storing vocabulary
Game	Wordsnake

LEARNING TO LEARN

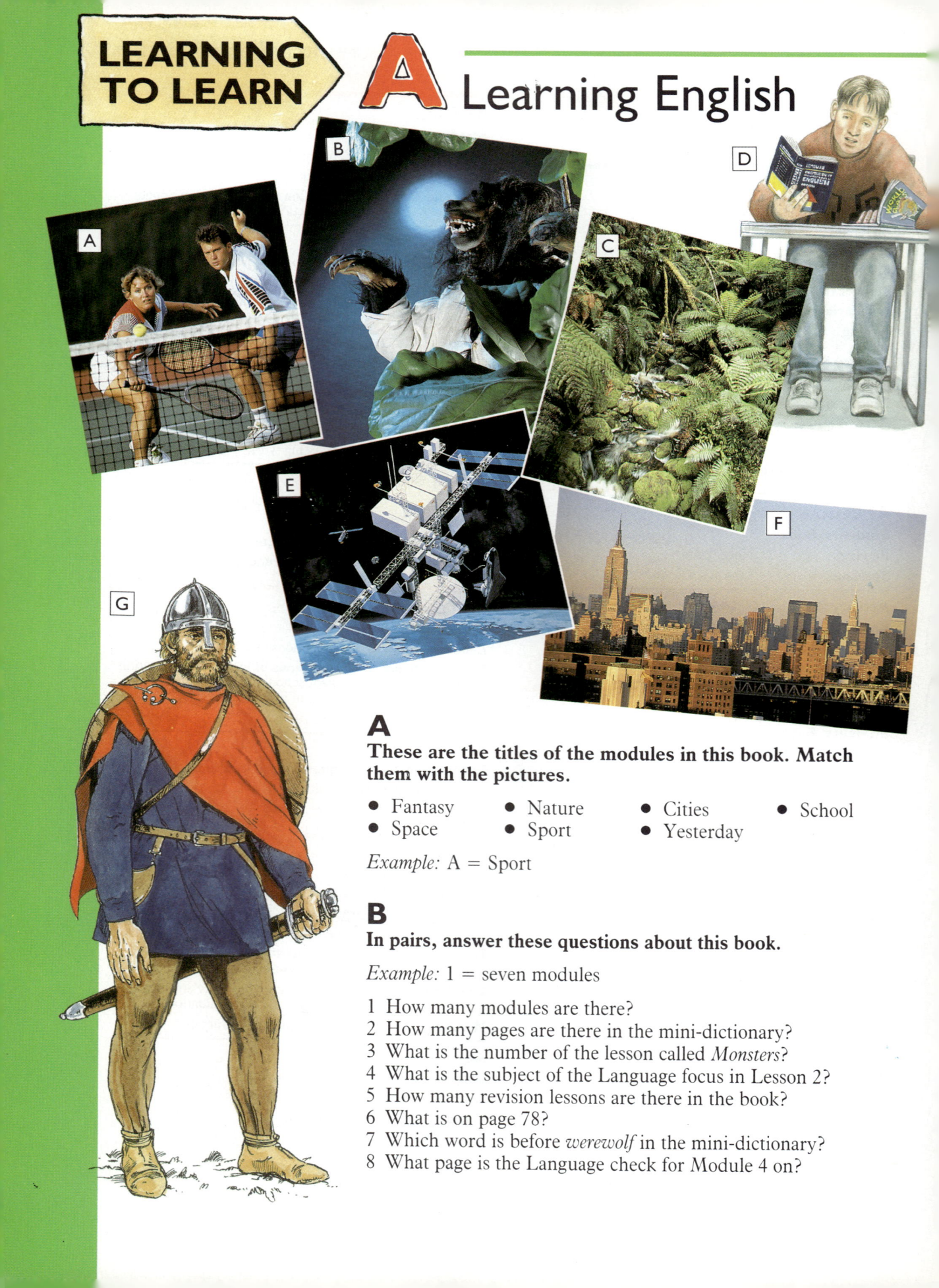

A Learning English

A
These are the titles of the modules in this book. Match them with the pictures.

- Fantasy
- Nature
- Cities
- School
- Space
- Sport
- Yesterday

Example: A = Sport

B
In pairs, answer these questions about this book.

Example: 1 = seven modules

1 How many modules are there?
2 How many pages are there in the mini-dictionary?
3 What is the number of the lesson called *Monsters*?
4 What is the subject of the Language focus in Lesson 2?
5 How many revision lessons are there in the book?
6 What is on page 78?
7 Which word is before *werewolf* in the mini-dictionary?
8 What page is the Language check for Module 4 on?

LEARNING TO LEARN

C
In pairs, interview your partner and find out if he/she is a good student.

1. **Do you try to speak English in the class?**
   a) usually
   b) never
   c) sometimes

2. **When the teacher says something that you don't understand, what do you do?**
   a) ask the teacher to repeat in your language
   b) say nothing
   c) ask another student
   d) ask the teacher to repeat in English

3. **When you come to the class what do you bring?**
   a) nothing
   b) your book and a piece of paper
   c) your book, activity book, notebook and a dictionary

4. **Which of these things do you try to do outside the class?**
   a) listen to songs in English
   b) read stories in English
   c) write to a penfriend in English
   d) watch films in English

SCORES
1. a) = 3 b) = 0 c) = 1
2. a) = 1 b) = 0 c) = 1 d) = 3
3. a) = 0 b) = 1 c) = 3
4. 2 points for each answer

RESULTS
13 – 17 You are an excellent student. You will learn a lot this year!
6 – 12 You are a good student. But think about your learning. What else can you do to improve your English?
under 6 You are waiting for someone to 'teach' you English. Remember, it is you who has to learn!

D
Where do *you* hear or see English outside your class?

Example: I sometimes hear foreign tourists speaking English in my own town.

foreign tourists / the cinema / videos / pop songs / television / newspapers / magazines / comics / labels or names of products / advertising / instructions / books / radio

E
Listen to a teacher replying to eight questions from students. What do you think the questions were?

Example: 1 How do you spell *dictionary*?

Listen again and check your answers.

F
In pairs, use the questions from exercise E to test your partner about the words below.

Example: A: How do you spell cupboard?
B: C–U–P–B–O–A–R–D.

cupboard / dictionary / pencil / bag / desk / ruler / glue / scissors / notebook / blackboard / pencil sharpener / homework / wastepaper basket / classroom

B A star

A

In groups, ask and answer about favourite film stars, singers and favourite sports people.

B

In pairs, put the instructions for reading in order.

Example: 1 = a

a) First look at the illustrations and guess what the text is about.
b) This time don't use the mini-dictionary.
c) Next, read it a second time to get more information.
d) Then look at the text and guess where it is from (magazine, book, etc.).
e) This time use the mini-dictionary for important words.
f) After that, read through it very quickly to get basic information.

C

Do steps 1, 2 and 3 from exercise B for the text on the right. Copy and complete the table.

Subject	Kevin Costner
Where from	....
Age of person	....
Job	....
Family	....
Likes	....

D

Read it again and answer the questions.

1 Where did Kevin Costner grow up?
2 What jobs has he had?
3 Which film won the Golden Globe award?
4 How does he feel about his family?

KEVIN

[1] Kevin Costner is one of the most famous <u>stars</u> of Hollywood. He was born in 1956 and grew up in
[5] California. Kevin went to Villa Park High School. He was an average student, but he was very good at sport. After high school,
[10] Kevin went to Fullerton University where he got a degree in business studies. He also started acting classes.
[15]   Kevin graduated from university in 1978, but could not get a full-time job. So he did all sorts of jobs. He was a truck
[20] driver and a carpenter and a tourist guide. But he felt he was born to act so he got a job as a stage hand. Stage hands are
[25] the people who move the scenery around.
   The first film that Kevin

4

LEARNING TO LEARN

COSTNER

acted in was called *Night Shift* (1982). His next film
30 was called *No Way Out* (1987), quickly followed by *The Untouchables* (1987). Kevin's first real <u>hit</u> was when he <u>played</u>
35 the part of Robin Hood. Robin Hood was a famous English outlaw who stole from the rich and gave to the poor. His next film,
40 *Dances with Wolves*, won the Golden Globe award. In this film he <u>starred</u> as an American army officer who makes friends with
45 Sioux Indians. Costner plays John Dunbar who the Indians call 'Dances with Wolves'.

Kevin Costner is now
50 very rich and famous, but success has not gone to his head. He is a home loving man and is very <u>close</u> to his family. His
55 wife's name is Cindy and they have three children: Annie, Lily and Joe.

Kevin likes sport and keeping fit. One thing is
60 certain about Kevin Costner, his future career should be interesting to watch.

E
Use the mini-dictionary to find the correct definition of these words:

star (*line* 2) / hit (*line* 34) / played (*line* 34)
starred (*line* 42) / close (*line* 54)

Example: hit = *noun* a film or song which everybody likes

F
Which of these things can help *you* remember new words?

1 Select only the important new words when you are reading.
2 Write down new words on pieces of paper.
3 Write down important new words in a vocabulary book.
4 Write down all the new words you see.
5 Include information about their form (*noun/adjective/verb*).
6 Translate words into your language.
7 Write down an example sentence.
8 Do vocabulary networks like this:

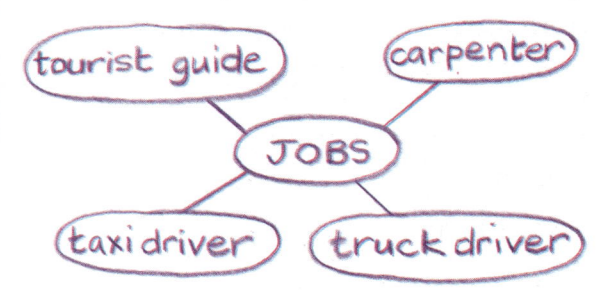

```
( tourist guide )        ( carpenter )
            \            /
            ( JOBS )
            /            \
( taxi driver )         ( truck driver )
```

G
Organise your vocabulary book. Label the pages alphabetically. Decide how many pages to leave for each letter. Then write down important new words from this lesson. Include this information:

career - n. (noun) = a person's working life
Example: Kevin Costner's future career will be interesting to watch.

5

C Your life

A

In pairs, which of these statements about listening to English do you agree with?

1. Some people are more difficult to understand than others.
2. You have to understand every word.
3. You need to use your dictionary when listening.
4. It is useful to guess what you are going to hear before you listen.
5. Often you only need to understand a part of what you hear.
6. It is easier to understand someone when you can see them speaking.

B

Look at the two photos. How old are they? Where do you think they come from? Listen to the cassette and find out.

C

Copy this table. Listen again and complete it for Maureen and Winston.

	Maureen	Winston	Your partner
Gets up		6.30	
Finishes school			
After school	*homework / reading*		
Weekends		*swimming / playing cricket*	

D

In pairs, find out about your partner's life and complete the table.

Example: What time do you get up?

E
Read the letter and correct the mistakes.

Example: My sister ~~start~~ *started* university at Leyden last year.

22 Heerenstraat,
Uden,
The Netherlands

13th February

Dear Alicia,

I am your new penfriend. My name is Tjeerd and I am from Holland. I am fourteen years old and I have got one sister and one brother. My sister <u>start</u> university at Leyden last year and she <u>is not live</u> at home at the moment. My brother <u>work</u> in a computer company. I am still at school but I want to study languages at university. This summer I am <u>going study</u> Spanish in Salamanca.

I don't like sport very much and my favourite hobby in the winter is playing with my computer. In the summer I go sailing with my father and my brother. Last year we <u>win</u> a race from Enkhuizen to Hoorn! There are quite a few things I don't like, for example getting up early and my maths teacher!

What is Venezuela like? <u>I have visit</u> quite a few places in Europe but never South America. Write to me soon and tell me all about yourself!

Best wishes,
Tjeerd

F
List examples of these tenses in the corrected letter:

- Present simple
- Present continuous
- Future with *going to*
- Past simple
- Present perfect

Example: Present simple = I don't like sport very much.

G
Tense game. In groups, one person chooses a verb and a tense and the next gives an example. If you can't give an example or your example is wrong, you are out of the game!

Example: A: get up – past simple.
B: I got up yesterday. Present continuous.
C: My sister getting up now.
A, B: No . . . wrong. She is getting up now.

Use these verbs:

get up / study / live / work / visit / play / speak / learn / watch

MODULE 1
CITIES

Great cities

1 Cairo, on the impressive River Nile, is a fascinating city of great contrasts. Arabs founded the city in 641, and it has been the centre of Egypt for centuries. Now it is the largest city in Africa, a busy city full of character, with an exciting mixture of ancient and modern.
Places to see: In the city there are many magnificent mosques and you can visit the Egyptian Museum to see the wonderful treasures of Tutankhamen. Outside Cairo are the Sphinx and the monumental pyramids, one of the Seven Wonders of the World.
On the menu: Try specialities like kebabs. Finish off your meal in style with some delicious sweet coffee.

2 Mysterious Cuzco is over three thousand metres high, in the Andes mountains in Peru. It was the prosperous capital of the powerful Inca Empire, which stretched from Colombia to Chile. The Spanish conquered it in 1533, but in historic Cuzco you can still feel the atmosphere of the ancient Inca civilisation.
Places to see: Walk along the ancient streets of Cuzco among the impressive Spanish colonial buildings. Visit the Inca ruins of the Temple of the Sun, or go on a trip to the wonderful lost city of Machu Picchu near Cuzco.
On the menu: Try out some tasty *papas a la huancaina* (potatoes with a cheese sauce). For the main course have some lovely roast lamb.

A
In groups, play the City Game. One student names a city (in the world or in his/her country). The others name cities beginning with the same letter.

Example: A: Casablanca
B: Cairo
C: Caracas
D: Canberra
E: Copenhagen
F: Cuzco
G: I don't know! (out of the game)

B
Look at the cities in the brochure. Which one would you like to visit?

C
Read the brochure carefully. Are these statements true or false?

1 Cairo is the largest city in Africa.
2 You can see the Sphinx in the Egyptian Museum.
3 Cuzco is the centre of a big empire.
4 Venice was a very rich city.
5 *Tartufo* is a kind of coffee.

3 The beautiful city of Venice is built on water which gives it a magical and romantic atmosphere. Merchants founded the city on small islands near to the coast and it became very rich and important. The merchants of Venice spent their money building magnificent buildings.

Places to see: Start off in the superb St Mark's Square and walk around this relaxing and peaceful city (there are no cars!). You will come across many impressive palaces, churches and bridges.

On the menu: Try the lovely seafood and you can look forward to *tartufo*, a rich chocolate and vanilla ice cream, for a delicious dessert.

D

Read the texts again. Find two adjectives describing each city.

Example: Cairo – fascinating / busy

Then find three adjectives describing buildings and three describing food. How many of the adjectives are similar in your language? Use the mini-dictionary to check the meanings.

E LEARN TO LEARN

Match these verbs from the text with the definitions.

1 finish off   a) to expect to enjoy something
2 start off   b) to test something by experience
3 try out   c) to discover something by chance
4 come across d) to conclude / to end
5 look forward to e) to begin

Now use the mini-dictionary to check your answers.

F

Read the postcard from Venice. Check the information with the tourist brochure and find five facts that are wrong.

Example: Venice isn't in Egypt.

> Venice, August 16th
>
> Dear Mum,
> Am having a great time here in Egypt! At the moment am in Venice, on the river Nile. Have been to the impressive pyramids and to St Mark's Square. Have also eaten lots of lovely pasta called 'tartufo'. Tomorrow going to see the lost city of Machu Picchu.
>
> Mrs J. K. Weinburger,
> 234 Main Street,
> Little Rock
> Arkansas
> USA

G

Look at the postcard again. What words are not included?

Example: (I) am having a great time.

Write a postcard from Cairo or Cuzco.

Stage 1 Write short notes about the city.

    Example: Cairo = pyramids/museum/Nile

Stage 2 Draw the back of a postcard.
Stage 3 Use your notes to write the postcard.

9

2 On tour

A

Look at the map of Europe. Plan your personal tour of six cities.

Example: London   Paris   Venice   Rome
                Madrid   Lisbon

B

Listen to Sophie Caldwell talking about her tour. Answer the questions.

1 Where is she now?
2 Does she like the city?
3 Has Sophie ever been on tour before?

C

Listen again and complete the sentences.

She has already been to Milan, ... ,
. . . . . , ... and . . . . .
She still has not been to Madrid, ... ,
. . . . . and . . . . .

Language focus:

PRESENT PERFECT WITH *STILL / YET / ALREADY*

D

Look at these sentences from the interview.

'We've *already* been to Rome and Prague.'
'Have you been to Paris *yet*?'
'We haven't been to Madrid *yet*.'
'We *still* haven't been to Barcelona and Lisbon.'

Which word do we use with affirmative, negative and questions with the present perfect? Complete the table.

Affirmative	....
Negative	....
Questions	....

Which of these words do we use:
a) between the subject and the auxiliary?
b) between the auxiliary and the main verb?
c) at the end of the sentence?

10

Map showing: Amsterdam, Prague, Vienna, Budapest, Milan, Venice, Rome

E

Imagine you are on your tour of Europe (from exercise A). Decide where you are now and write sentences about the cities.

Examples: I've already been to London.
I haven't been to Amsterdam yet.
I still haven't been to Rome.

F

In pairs, find out the cities on your partner's tour.

Example: A: Have you been to Venice yet?
B: No, I haven't been there yet. I'm going there tomorrow. / I still haven't been there. / I've already been there. / I'm not going there. (*if a city is not on your tour*)

Language focus:
PAST SIMPLE / PRESENT PERFECT

G

Look at the questions and answers in the box. Past simple or present perfect?

> 1 'Have you ever been to America?'
> 'Yes, I have.'
> 2 'When did you go there?'
> 'I went there last year.'

H

Write a list of places you have visited in your country. Write when you visited them.

Example: Rio de Janeiro 1991 / São Paulo 1990 / Manáus 1989

In pairs, find out where your partner has been and when he/she went there.

Example: A: Have you ever been to Manáus?
B: Yes, I have. (*or* No, I haven't.)
A: When did you go there?
B: In 1989.

I

Travel game. In groups of four, think of places in your country. Say you've been there. If you can't think of a real place you are out of the game.

Example: A: I've been to Rio de Janeiro.
B: What did you see/do there?
A: I went to the beach at Copacabana. Where have you been?

Amazing but true!

Venice is built on 118 small islands. There are over 400 bridges crossing the canals.

3 Lifestyles

A
Where do you live? In a big city, a small town or a country village?
Where do you think Larry and Jane live?
Listen to the conversation and find out.
Which place would you prefer to live in?

B
Copy the table. Listen and complete it for Larry and Jane.

	Larry	Jane
Going out		
Eating out		*pizzas*
At weekends	*fishing / swimming*	
After school		

C
Listen again. Look at the words below and list the advantages and disadvantages of both cities.

crime / shops / discos / sports / traffic / restaurants / buildings / pollution / cinema / noise

New York		York	
Disadvantages	Advantages	Disadvantages	Advantages
crime (−)	*shops* (+)	*shops* (−)	*sports* (+)

D
Copy the table in exercise B again. In groups, interview two other people and complete it.

Example: A: Where do you go when you go out?
B: I go to the cinema.

E
In pairs, list the advantages and the disadvantages of living in the city or the country.

Example: In the city the shops are good.
In the country there aren't many . . .

F

Read the description of Madrid. Which paragraph describes:

- advantages?
- disadvantages?
- basic information?

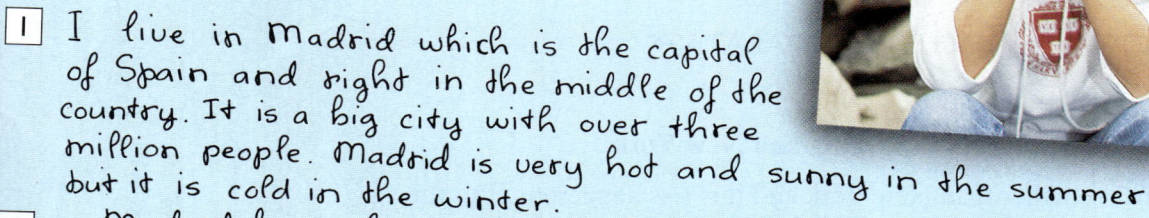

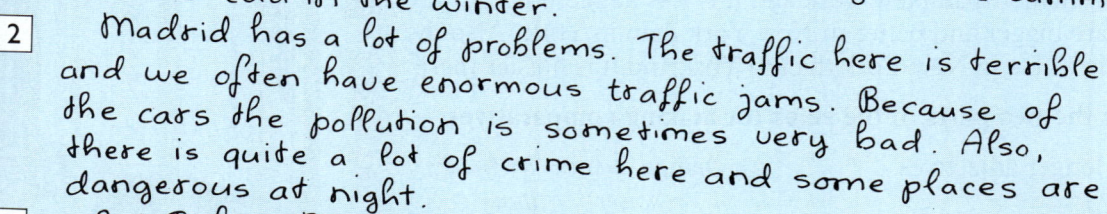

1 I live in Madrid which is the capital of Spain and right in the middle of the country. It is a big city with over three million people. Madrid is very hot and sunny in the summer but it is cold in the winter.

2 Madrid has a lot of problems. The traffic here is terrible and we often have enormous traffic jams. Because of the cars the pollution is sometimes very bad. Also, there is quite a lot of crime here and some places are dangerous at night.

3 But I love Madrid and there are lots of good things. The people are friendly and the city is never boring. There are lots of things to do and places to go. In the summer we live out of doors and nobody goes to bed early. Madrid is probably the only place in the world which has traffic jams at four or five o'clock in the morning!

G

Copy the table below. Read the description again and decide in which paragraphs you find information about these things:

- traffic
- location
- people
- population
- places to go
- pollution
- weather
- life in the summer
- crime

Description of Madrid: Plan

Paragraph 1: Location

Paragraph 2:

Paragraph 3:

Cities project

H

Write a description of your city or a city you know.

Stage 1 Write notes like those in exercise G.
Stage 2 Use the notes to write a description (with three paragraphs).
Stage 3 Show your description to your partner and look at his/hers. Can you see any mistakes in your partner's description? Can he/she see any in yours?
Stage 4 Write a final version of your description.

Keep this description for the project in Lesson 7.

4 Old and new

A
Look at the two photos of York and New York. Think of differences between the two cities.

Example: New York: big / dangerous   York: small / safe

Language focus: COMPARATIVES

B
Read this description of York and New York

York is smaller than New York and it is less dangerous. But the shops are bigger and better in New York than in York. Also the traffic is worse in New York than in York and it is noisier there.

Match the two parts of the rules for making comparatives.

1 For longer adjectives   a) change -y into -ier (*noisy = noiser*) + *than*

2 For adjectives ending in -y   b) add -er (*small = smaller*) + *than*

3 For short adjectives   c) change completely (*good = better*)

4 For irregular adjectives   d) use *more* or *less* + adjective (*dangerous = more/less dangerous*)

C
Copy the tables below and classify these adjectives.

small / noisy / good / big / modern / relaxing / new / friendly / hot / sunny / safe / boring / romantic / busy / impressive / old

Look through this module and add other adjectives.

Short adjectives	
small	smaller
noisy	noisier
big	bigger*

Long adjectives	
modern	more/less modern

Irregular adjectives	
good	better

* Look at the change of spelling

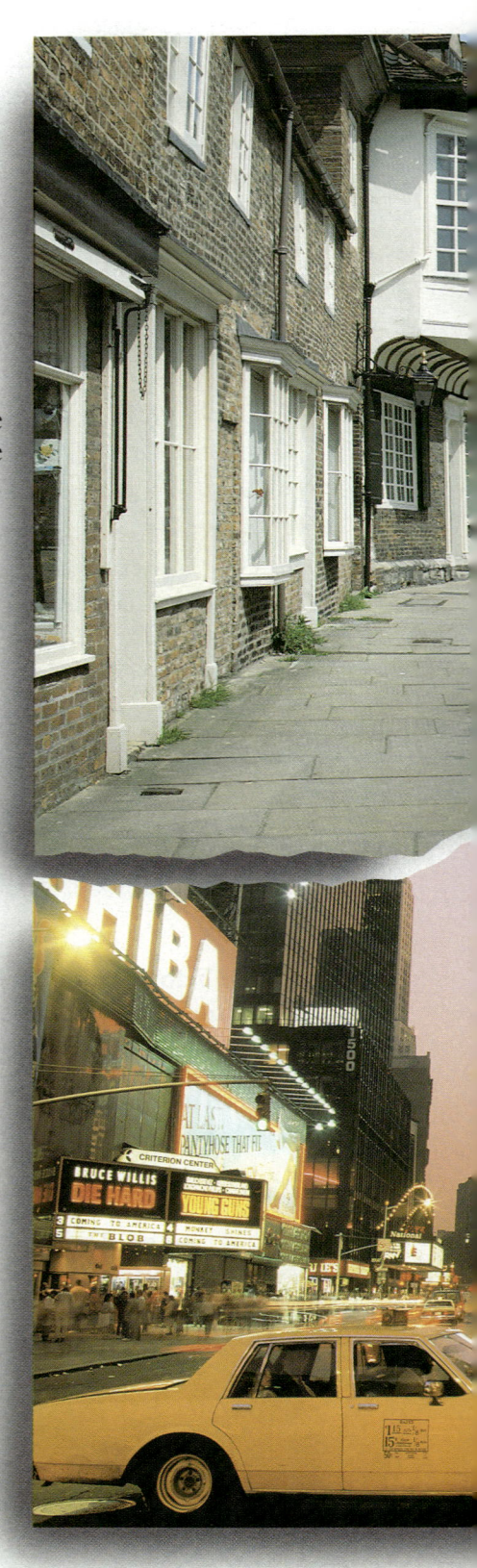

D

Write three sentences comparing where you live with York or New York.

Example: Size: It is smaller than New York.

E

Guess the name of this North American city.

> It is bigger in area than New York. The streets are more dangerous than Beirut. The pollution is worse than London. It is warmer in winter than Rome. There are more film stars than any other city in the world. It has got a Spanish name and more people speak Spanish than English.

Now choose a city in your own country and write a similar description. Don't put the name!

F

Guessing game. Read out your descriptions to the rest of the class. The first pair to guess the city wins.

Pronunciation

G

Copy the words and then listen and mark the main stress.

bigger / important / smaller / noisier / mysterious
dirtier / healthier / warmer / modern /
magnificent / better / delicious / enormous

Example: bigger, important

Now listen again and mark the sound /ə/.

Example: bigger, important

Amazing but true!

In 1626, a Dutchman bought some land for $24 from the local Indians and founded a town called New Amsterdam. That town is now called New York.

15

5 Getting around

A
Which of these types of texts do you read in your own language? Which do you read in English? Which are more difficult? In pairs, put them in order of difficulty.

- magazine articles
- books (fiction)
- books (facts)
- tourist brochures
- notices
- newspapers
- letters
- postcards

B
Where does the text below come from? Match the photos with the paragraphs.

Example: A = 3

Global traffic jam

How long does it take you to get to school in the mornings? In some big cities it can take ages to go anywhere and millions of people spend hours sitting in traffic jams. For example, in Lima in Peru, the traffic is so bad during the rush hour that it is quicker to walk than to go by bus or car.

Pollution danger
2 The problem with walking to school is that you have to breathe, and in many cities the air is not exactly clean. In some cities the pollution caused by cars is so dangerous that people wear masks in the street.

No cars
3 There are very few cities with no cars. Venice is one of these and people get around on foot or by boat, by water buses or water taxis. It is more expensive to go by gondola and not very fast, but much more romantic!

Public transport
4 In many places public transport also gets very crowded in rush hours. In Tokyo there are special workers to push people into the underground trains. But if you go by underground you can avoid traffic jams and public transport causes less pollution.

On your bike!
5 Perhaps the best way of getting around is by getting on your bike. It can be more dangerous but a lot of cities have special bicycle lanes. Going by bike does not cause any pollution and it is good exercise for you!

C
Read the text again. Copy and complete the table.

Transport	Advantages	Disadvantages
Car	–	traffic jams / pollution
Underground		
Gondola		
Bicycle		

16

D

In groups, find out about other people's transport.

Example: A: How do you get to school?   B: On foot.
A: How long does it take you?   B: Twenty minutes.

Report the results of your group.

Example: Two people come by car and two by bus. The average time it takes us is fifteen minutes.

E

Complete this dialogue at a London tourist office.

A: Excuse me?
B: I'm sorry, just a moment please. (*pause*) Yes, can I help you?
A: Can you give me information about getting around [1] . . . . . on the underground please?
B: Well, here's a [2] . . . . . showing the different lines.
A: Thank you. What about tickets? Are they expensive?
B: Mmm, it depends on the distance. But you can get a [3] . . . . . day travel card. They cost [4] . . . . . pounds sixty.
A: Thanks very much.

Listen and check your answers.

Pronunciation

F

Copy the dialogue and listen again. Mark the intonation at the end of the sentences. Does it go up or down?

Example: A: Excuse me?   B: I'm sorry, just a moment please.

G

Work in pairs. Student A, imagine you are a tourist in your town. Student B, you work in the tourist information office. Act out this situation. Use the correct intonation!

A: Ask for help	B: Reply
A: Ask for information about buses	B: Give a map / timetable
A: Ask about the numbers of buses	B: Give information
A: Ask about price of tickets	B: Give information
A: Ask about times of buses	B: Give information

17

6 Going out

A
Look at the photos and list the activities.

Example: A = going to the cinema

Cities project

B

In pairs, make a list of things to do for young people where you live. Give names of places, times they are open and how to get there.

Example: Dancing: The Zone, young discotheque, open 5.00 – 9.00 pm Sat/Sun (bus)
Swimming: Olympic Pool, open 9.00 am – 8.00 pm (underground)

18

C

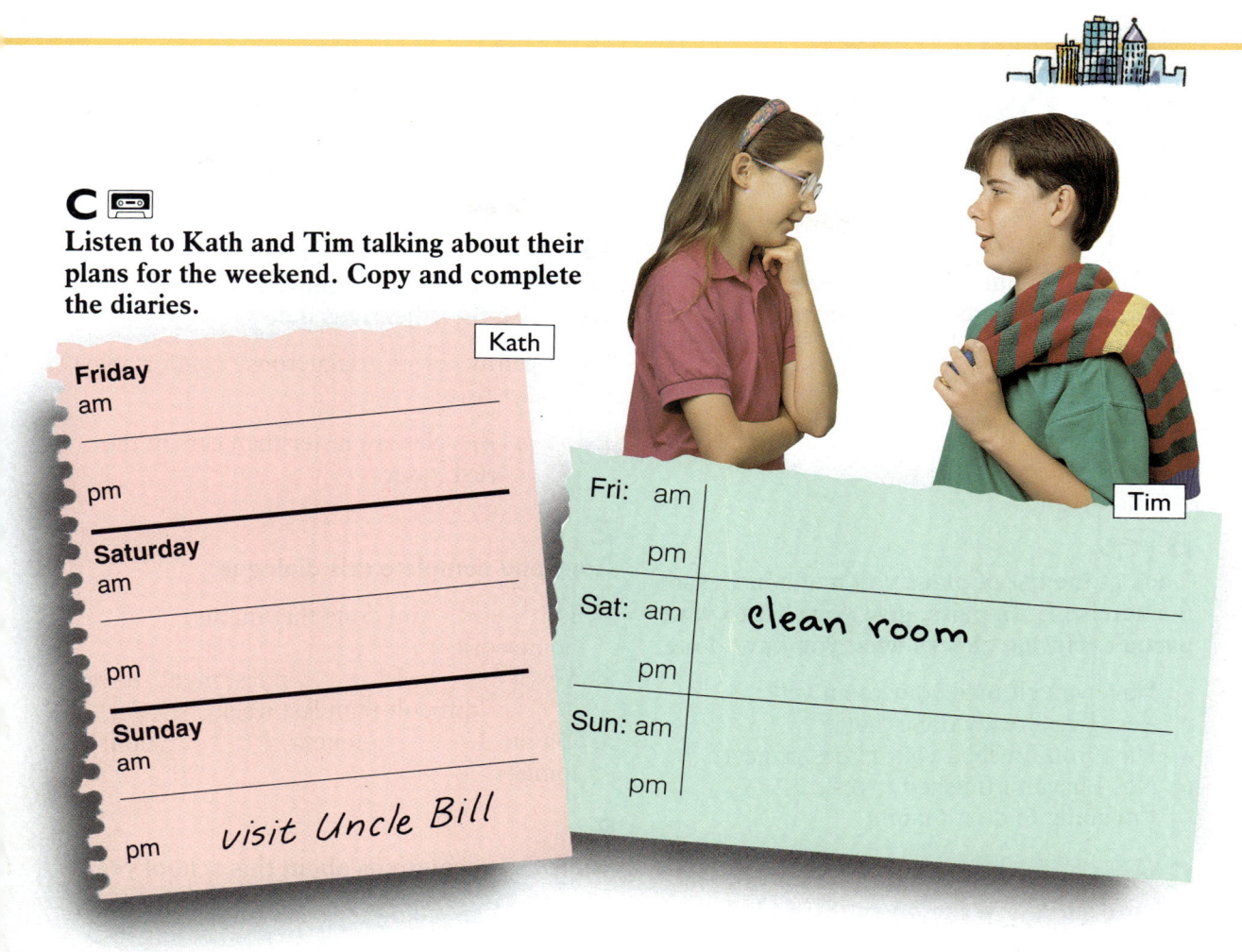

Listen to Kath and Tim talking about their plans for the weekend. Copy and complete the diaries.

Kath

Friday
am
pm

Saturday
am
pm

Sunday
am
pm visit Uncle Bill

Tim

Fri: am
pm
Sat: am clean room
pm
Sun: am
pm

Language focus: PLANS AND INTENTIONS

D
Match the rules with the examples.

1 We use the present simple to write plans in a diary.	a) I'm going to clean my room! It's in a terrible mess!
2 We use *going to* to talk about plans and intentions (things important for us to do).	b) Tonight I'm meeting Paul and we're going to the cinema.
3 We use the present continuous to talk about arrangements at specific times and with verbs of movement.	c) visit Uncle Bill

E
Write five sentences about things you plan to do next weekend.

Example: I'm going to buy some records.

F
Write definite plans in diary form.

Example: Fri. 4pm: go shopping in the Avon Centre with Susan

G
In pairs, find out what your partner is doing at the weekend.

Example: A: What are you doing on Friday afternoon?
B: At four o'clock I'm going shopping with Susan in the Avon Centre.

7 Revision

Listening

A

Listen to this quiz. You will hear descriptions of five cities. Can you identify the city before the contestants? All the cities are from this module.

Example: 1 = York

Speaking

B

Look at the list of plans you made in Lesson 6, exercise E. In pairs, give your list to your partner. He/she checks what you have done.

A: Have you cleaned your room yet?
B: Yes, I've already done that.
A: Have you finished your Cities project?
B: No, I haven't finished it yet.
 I'm going to do it tonight.

C

Leisure survey. Write down three kinds of entertainment.

Example: football match / pop concert / circus

In groups, find out who has been to these and when they went.

Example:
A: Have you ever been to a football match?
B: Yes, I have.
A: When did you go?
B: Last year . . . in June, I think.

Write down the results of the survey, like this:

1988		
June '90		
Aug '91		1987
June '92	May '92	June '91
football match	pop concert	circus

Language revision

D

Write five sentences comparing bicycles and cars. Use the adjectives below.

fast / healthy / clean / dangerous / comfortable / safe / expensive

Example: Bicycles are faster than cars in the rush hour.

E

Copy and complete this dialogue.

A: Hi! ^{1}..... you done that maths homework ^{2}.....?
B: Yes, I ^{3}..... I ^{4}..... it last night. It was ^{5}..... difficult than last week.
A: Oh no! I ^{6}..... done it. I ^{7}..... do it tonight.

F

Make five resolutions about this school year.

Example: I am going to speak English all the time in class.

Learner training

G

Which of these words are similar in your language?

Example: German: cold = *kalt*
 friend = *freund*
 come = *kommen*

cold / empire / friend / temple / pyramid / airport / map / coffee / menu / come / traffic / magnificent / international / taxi / mosque / pasta / ballet / transport / crime / temperature / bicycle

Look at the reading text in Lesson 1 and add other words to your list.

H   Learn to learn

Look at the structures in the Language check. Use the ideas below to organise your own grammar notes in your notebook.

1 Table

Short adjectives

| São Paulo | is | bigger / noisier | than | York. |

2 Timeline

| Past | Present Perfect | Present |
| I went there in 1991 | I have already finished | Now |

Past Simple

3 Translation

I am going to the cinema.
(Gom Krakatoatri og chimimatik.)
I have already been there.
(Glogsti arg bodu gom gugu.)

Cities project

I

Write a guide for someone coming to your city.

Stage 1   Collect the information you have about where you live. Look for pictures in brochures or draw them yourself.
Stage 2   Think of other information that is useful – for example, festivals.
Stage 3   Write notes about these things.
Stage 4   Plan the presentation of the information (brochure / poster).
Stage 5   Use all your notes to write each part of the guide.
Stage 6   Add your personal description and the pictures.

J

Look at the Module check on page 107.

Language check

PRESENT PERFECT WITH STILL / YET / ALREADY

Have you been to Venice **yet**?
I have **already** been to Budapest.
I haven't been to Lisbon **yet**.
I **still** haven't been to Barcelona.

PRESENT PERFECT / PAST SIMPLE

Have you ever been to New York?
Yes, I **have**.
When **did you go** there?
I **went** there in 1991.

COMPARATIVES

Short adjectives
Rome is **older than** York.
Los Angeles is **bigger than** San Francisco.

Long adjectives
London is **less peaceful than** York, and it is **more dangerous**.

Irregular adjectives
The shops in London are **better than** those in York.

PLANS AND INTENTIONS

Plans
I **am seeing** Paul this evening.
My uncle **is flying** to London tomorrow.
I **am going to have** lunch at home today.

Written plans
(in diary)
go to the cinema with Paul

Intentions
I **am going to study** a lot on Sunday.
I **am going to put** important new words in my vocabulary book.

MODULE 2
YESTERDAY
8 Living in the past

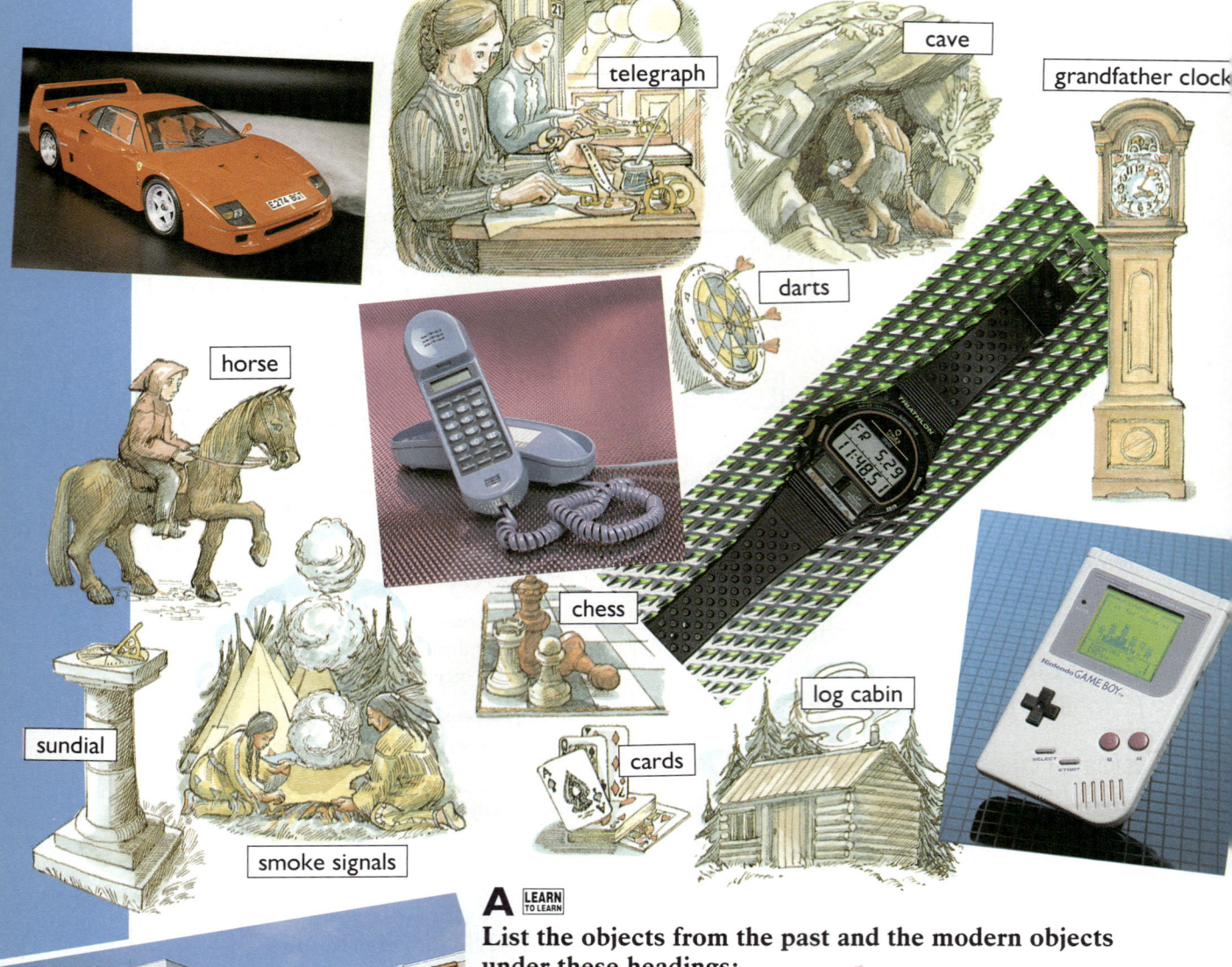

telegraph
cave
grandfather clock
darts
horse
chess
log cabin
sundial
smoke signals
cards
canoe

A LEARN TO LEARN
List the objects from the past and the modern objects under these headings:

- communication
- telling the time
- transport
- homes
- games

B
In groups, take turns to say a sentence. The others say if it's true or false.

Example: A: People lived in log cabins before they lived in caves.
B, C and D: False
B: People played chess before they played video games.
A, C and D: True

C

In groups, look at this picture of some Vikings. What mistakes can you find?

Example: They didn't ride motorbikes.

D

In pairs, Student A looks at number 1 on page 108 and reads about Aztecs. Student B looks at number 1 on page 110 and reads about Vikings. Make notes for each heading in the diagram. You can use the mini-dictionary.

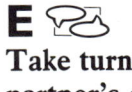

- FOOD
- GAMES
- TRANSPORT
- NAME OF PEOPLE
- DATES
- LOCATION
- WEAPONS

E

Take turns to ask questions about your partner's civilisation.

Example: What did they eat?

FOOD:	What / eat?
TRANSPORT:	How / travel?
LOCATION:	Where / live?
WEAPONS:	What / fight with?
DATES:	When / live?
GAMES:	What / play?

Did you know?

Rich people in Ancient Rome enjoyed enormous meals. Mice were a great delicacy!

9 History makers

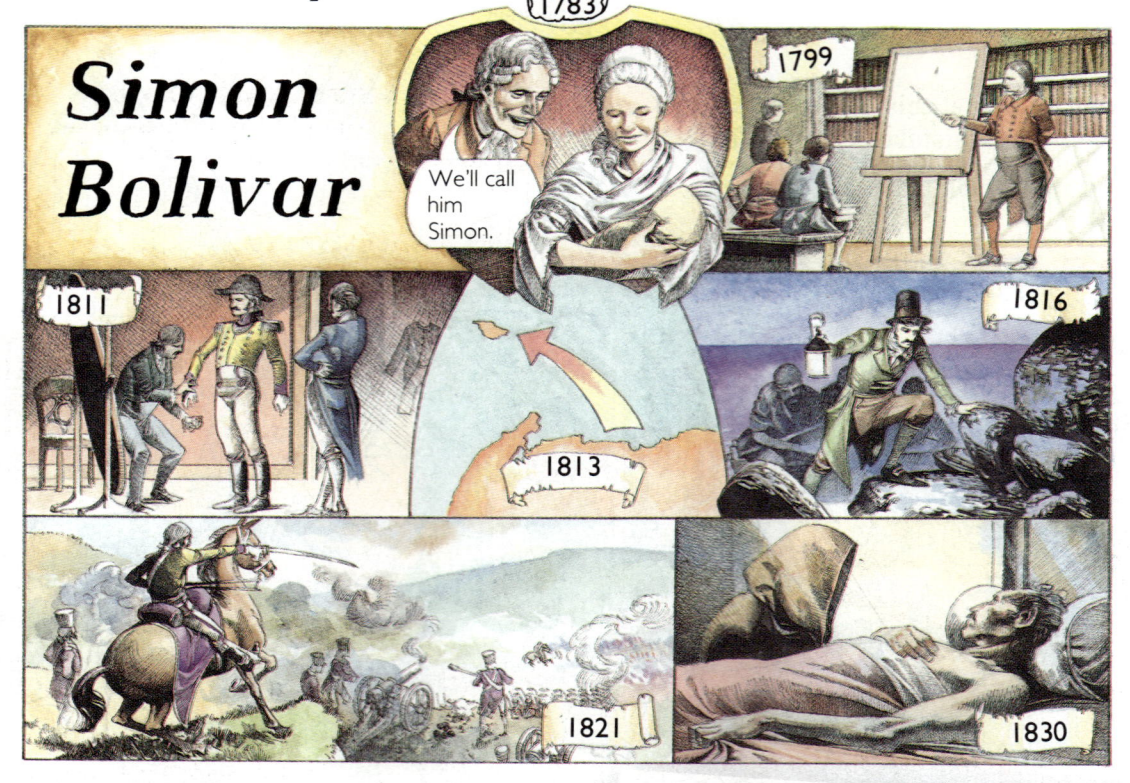

Simon Bolivar

"We'll call him Simon."

1783 / 1799 / 1811 / 1813 / 1816 / 1821 / 1830

A
Look at the picture story about Simon Bolivar. Match the pictures with the captions.

1 becomes General of the Venezuelan Army
2 dies
3 is born in Caracas
4 wins a battle and liberates Caracas
5 has to go to Jamaica to escape from the Spanish
6 secretly returns to Venezuela
7 goes to school in Europe

Language focus:
PAST SIMPLE – IRREGULAR VERBS

B
Read the text and fill in the gaps. Use the verbs below in the past simple.

go / return / die / be / have to / can / reorganise / fight / become / lose / defeat

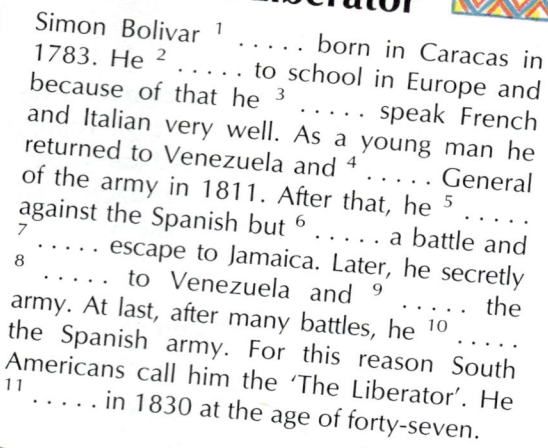

The Liberator

Simon Bolivar [1] ..... born in Caracas in 1783. He [2] ..... to school in Europe and because of that he [3] ..... speak French and Italian very well. As a young man he returned to Venezuela and [4] ..... General of the army in 1811. After that, he [5] ..... against the Spanish but [6] ..... a battle and [7] ..... escape to Jamaica. Later, he secretly [8] ..... to Venezuela and [9] ..... the army. At last, after many battles, he [10] ..... the Spanish army. For this reason South Americans call him the 'The Liberator'. He [11] ..... in 1830 at the age of forty-seven.

C
Look at the verbs in the text and answer these questions.

1 Which verbs are regular verbs? How do they end?
2 Which verb shows *obligation* in the past?
3 Which verb shows *ability* in the past?

D

Listen to the story of another 'History maker'. Put these verbs in the order you hear them.

Example: 1 = see

pass / see / meet / start / arrive / want / crash

Amy Johnson

E

Listen again. Are these sentences true or false?

1 Amy was quite poor.
2 She flew to America.
3 She could speak German.
4 She repaired her aeroplane in India.

F

Listen again and write down:

- two sentences which show obligation.
- one sentence which describes ability.

G

Here are some more people who made history. Match the photos with what they did. Can you name the people?

1 A great scientist who discovered radium.
2 The first woman in space.
3 A pacifist who fought for Indian independence.
4 A man who fought for the rights of black people in the USA.

H

Test your partner. In pairs, take turns to ask each other questions. Student A looks at number 2 on page 108 and Student B looks at number 2 on page 110.

25

10 King Arthur

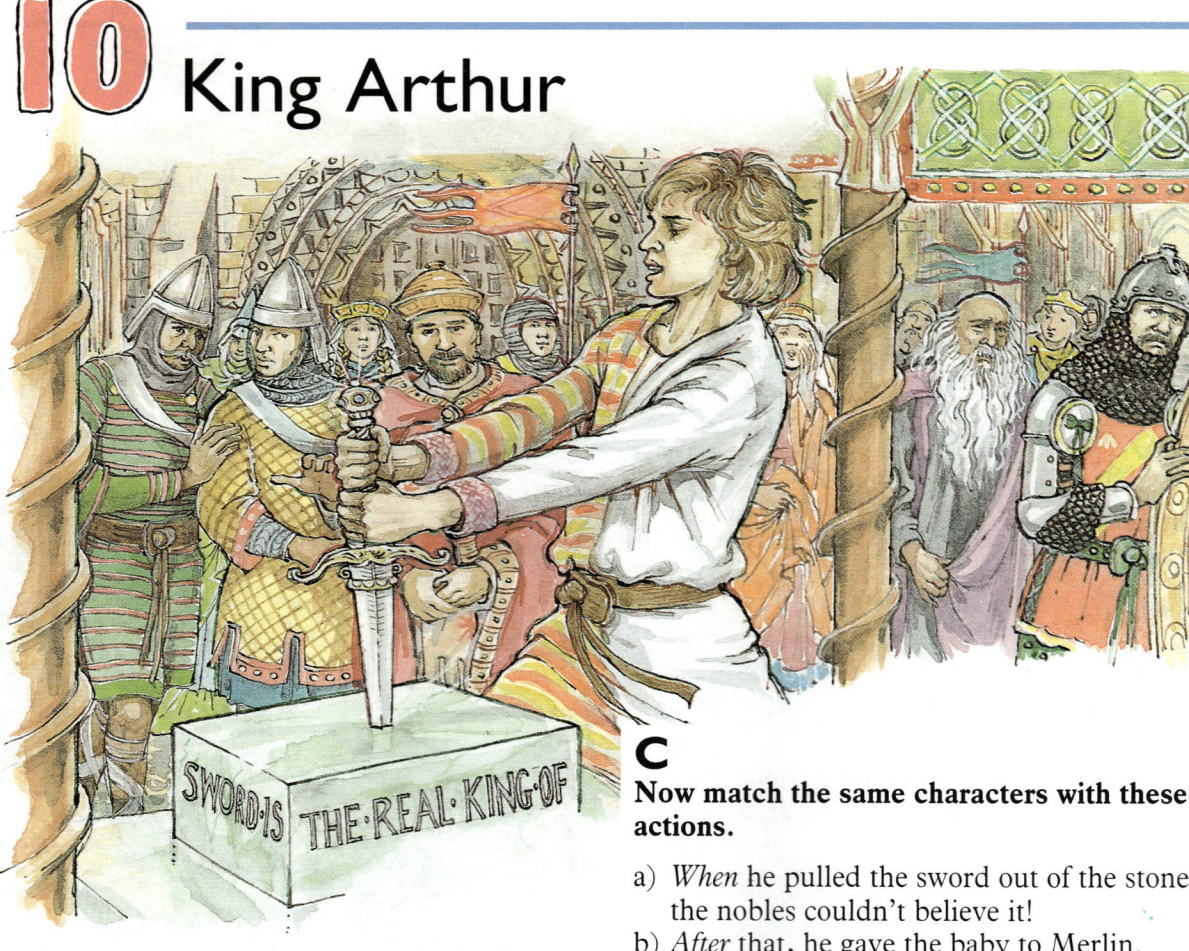

A
Listen to the story and put the characters in the order you hear about them.

Example: 1 = Pendragon

- Merlin the Wizard
- Young Arthur
- King Pendragon

B
Listen again and match the characters with the adjectives.

Merlin   happy and healthy
Arthur   brave but bad
King Pendragon wise

C
Now match the same characters with these actions.

a) *When* he pulled the sword out of the stone, the nobles couldn't believe it!
b) *After* that, he gave the baby to Merlin.
c) He fell in love with a noble's wife *and then* killed the noble.
d) *After* this, he explained everything and Arthur became king.
e) *When* he received the baby, he *immediately* sent him to a friend.
f) *Before* he went to London, he lived happily with Merlin's friend.
g) He got married. *Later*, his wife had a baby.

D
Put the sentences in exercise C in the correct order.

Example: 1 He fell in love with a noble's wife and then killed the noble.

Did you know?
Long ago, knights believed that a sword, dipped in dragon's blood, brought them good luck!

E
Use the words in *italics* from exercise C to complete the story.

Pendragon, the king, fell in love with the wife of a noble ¹____ killed the noble and married his wife. ²____ they had a baby son, Arthur, and gave him to the wizard Merlin. ³____ Merlin realised Arthur was in danger, he ⁴____ sent him to a friend. ⁵____ a few years, Pendragon died, and the nobles fought each other – they each wanted to be king. Merlin put a sword into a stone, with a message – 'The person who pulls out this sword is the real King of England.' ⁶____ the nobles tried, they couldn't do it.

⁷____, Arthur and his friend Kay went to a tournament in London. Kay forgot his sword and sent Arthur to get it. ⁸____ he could find Kay's sword, Arthur saw the sword in the stone and pulled it out. ⁹____ Kay saw it, he thought Arthur had stolen it and ¹⁰____ told him to put it back. Arthur did this, ¹¹____ Kay tried to pull the sword out, but he couldn't. Arthur ¹²____ pulled it out again. Arthur had to pull the sword out three more times ¹³____ the nobles believed he was the king. ¹⁴____ this, Merlin explained everything and Arthur became the King of England.

F
Make nouns from these adjectives. You can use the mini-dictionary.

happy / brave / healthy / wise

Example: happy – happiness

G
'Against the Clock' game. In pairs, each student writes down five adjectives from the mini-dictionary. Exchange lists. The first student to make nouns from the adjectives is the winner. Write down useful words in your vocabulary book.

Pronunciation

H
Listen to the different ways you can pronounce the letter 'i'.

Group 1	Group 2	Group 3
/aɪ/ time	/ɪ/ big	/ɜː/ girl

Mark each letter 'i' in these sentences 1, 2 or 3. Then listen and check your answers.

Example: They didn't find the rich girl.
                    2   1   2   3

1 They didn't find the rich girl.
2 First King Pendragon killed a noble.
3 Then his wife had a baby, Arthur.
4 After this, they gave him to Merlin, the wise wizard.

11 Memories

A
Les Hanlon was born in 1921. What do you think he will say about these things?

- first job
- family
- holidays
- free time
- living conditions
- school

B
Listen to Les talking about his childhood. Put the topics from exercise A in the order he talks about them.

C
Listen again. Are these sentences true or false?

1. We used to live next to a school.
2. I used to clean the rooms in the orphanage.
3. My teachers weren't very strict.
4. We used to have boxing tournaments.
5. We used to swim a lot in the summer.
6. I used to work in a coalmine.

Language focus: USED TO

D
Look at the sentences in the box and then answer the questions.

> 1 We *used to* have boxing tournaments.
> 2 I *didn't use to* play in the street.
> 3 Where did you *use to* live?

a) How does the spelling of *used to* change in negatives and questions?
b) Does *used to* refer to past or present habits?
c) What is the difference between:
   – I used to get up early.
   – I usually get up early.

E
Think about when you were five or six years old. Compare what you did then with your life now. Write about each of these things:

- homework
- bedtime
- food
- TV programmes
- sport
- lessons

Example: I didn't use to have any homework, but now I have some every day.
I used to go to bed at eight o'clock, but now I go much later.

F
In pairs, find out the same information from your partner.

Example:
A: Did you use to have a lot of homework?
B: No, I didn't use to have any homework.
A: And now?
B: Now I have homework every day.
A: What time did you use to go to bed?
B: About eight o'clock.

G
Now write three sentences about your partner.

Example: When she was young she used to go to bed early, but now she stays up late.

H
Ask your teacher some questions about his/her childhood.

Pronunciation

I
Listen to the six sentences. How many words are there in each sentence? Contractions, such as *what's*, count as two words.

Example: 1 = 7 words

Do you remember . . .
. . . your first day at school?
. . . the first film you saw at the cinema?
. . . your first holiday?
What is your earliest memory?

29

12 Hard times

A
Read the reports from 1842 and match each one with the correct drawing.

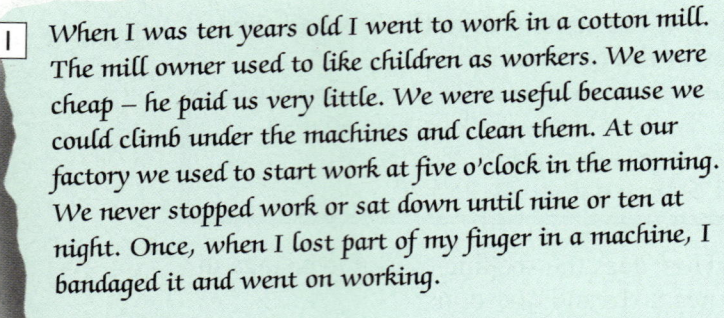

A

1 When I was ten years old I went to work in a cotton mill. The mill owner used to like children as workers. We were cheap – he paid us very little. We were useful because we could climb under the machines and clean them. At our factory we used to start work at five o'clock in the morning. We never stopped work or sat down until nine or ten at night. Once, when I lost part of my finger in a machine, I bandaged it and went on working.

(Boy, anonymous)

B

2 I don't get tired, but I'm frightened because I have a door without a candle. I never go to sleep. Sometimes I sing if there is light, but not in the dark. I don't dare sing then. I don't like being in the mine.

(Sarah Gooder, aged eight)

3 I go down the mine at five in the morning and I come up at five at night. I work all night on Fridays and come away at twelve in the morning. I carry coal to the bottom of the mine. It usually weighs seven stones[1]. The distance varies, sometimes 300 yards[2], sometimes 500 yards[3]. I have to bend my back and legs, and the water often comes up to my knees. I don't like the work; my father *makes* me like it.

(Janet Cumming, aged eleven)
1 about 45 kilos 2 about 277 metres 3 about 461 metres

C

4 When I was fourteen I started working for a family with nine children. I used to get up and light the fire, bath them and dress them, and get their breakfasts. Then I had to make the dinner and do all the washing up; and by that time, it would be teatime again. I had to put the children to bed, clean the rooms and prepare the fires for the next morning, and also the parents' supper. I wasn't in bed until twelve, and I had to get up by six.

(Susy, a domestic servant, aged sixteen)

D

B
Now answer these questions.

1 What time did Janet finish work on Saturdays?
2 How heavy was the coal that Janet carried?
3 How did Sarah feel when she was in the mine?
4 How many hours a day did children work in cotton mills?
5 How many meals did Susy have to prepare every day?

C
Read the texts again. Match the verbs on the left from the text with the definitions on the right. You can use the mini-dictionary.

1	go down (*text 3*)	a)	leave
2	come up (*text 3*)	b)	continued
3	come away (*text 3*)	c)	move to the bottom of the mine
4	comes up to (*text 3*)	d)	move to the top of the mine
5	went on (*text 1*)	e)	get out of bed
6	get up (*text 4*)	f)	reaches

D
In groups, discuss the questions below. Then report your answers to the class.

Example: 1 We think they liked them because they were cheap.

1 Why did mill owners like child workers?
2 How did you feel when you read the reports?
3 Which do you think is the worst of the four jobs?
4 Do you think the children knew how to read and write?
5 Why did so many children go to work?

E
In groups, prepare your own list of Children's Rights. They can be serious or amusing. Write at least five rights and then read them to the class.

Children's Rights
1. Children must have a good education to prepare them for life.
2. You mustn't go to school on your birthday.
3. There should be free doctors and dentists.
4. Children should have the right to watch TV when they want.

Pronunciation

F
In some words you don't pronounce a letter; some letters are silent. What are the silent letters in these words?

write / scientist / know / island / iron / scissors / sword / climb / answer

Listen and check your answers.

Did you know?
A horrible job for children in 19th century Britain was chimney-sweeping. Little boys had to climb inside chimneys to clean them.

31

13 Og

Og

Og: (population 1,250,000) Capital city of Ogland.

Roman building Temple of Rain

modern opera house

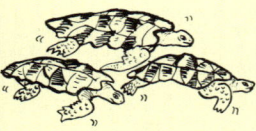

turtle racing scene

King Kevin I – early medieval warrior

1 **Og** is situated on the south coast of the island of Ogland. The city has grown a lot since the 1970s, when gold was discovered near the city. The old town has many interesting historic buildings including the magnificent Royal Palace and the ancient Temple of Rain. The Romans built that monumental building nearly 2,000 years ago. The new part of the city has changed a lot recently, with some impressive modern buildings like the new opera house and new parliament building. There are also many new hotels, department stores and office blocks.

2 There are two important festivals in Og. The winter games in January have skiing and skating events. Also famous are the enormous snowball fights between different groups of young Oggers in the streets of the city. On June 17th Og celebrates Independence Day, with street parties and sports including turtle racing and the incredibly dangerous shark riding competitions.

3 The Romans founded the city of Ogrium in 22 AD and occupied it for nearly four hundred years. Then the Vikings under Erik the Blue conquered the city. In 1007 the Oggers under King Kevin I defeated the Vikings at the battle of Ogsford. Ogland became independent and has been a neutral country for over six hundred years, since the end of the Anacondan wars in 1389. For centuries fishing and farming were the most important activities in Og. Everything changed in 1972, with the discovery of gold. Since then Og has become a prosperous and modern city.

A LEARN TO LEARN

The text above is from an encyclopedia. Which of these topics come before it, and which after it?

- Orinoco
- Oceania
- Olympic Games
- Ohio
- Odessa

B

Read the text quickly and match the paragraphs with these titles:

- History
- The city now
- Festivals

C
Copy and complete the diagram.

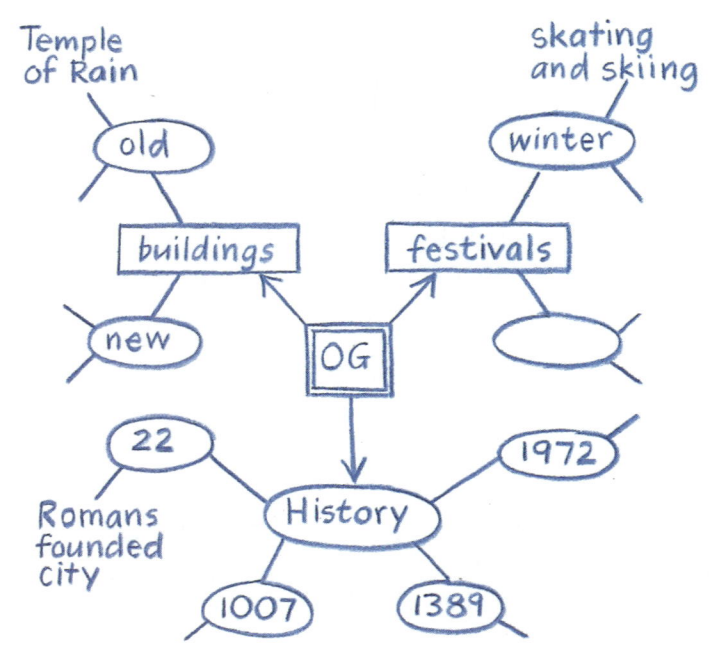

(Diagram: central node "OG" connecting to "buildings" (old → Temple of Rain; new), "festivals" (winter → skating and skiing; blank), and "History" (22 — Romans founded city; 1007; 1389; 1972))

Language focus: PAST SIMPLE / PRESENT PERFECT

D
In which of these sentences is there a link with the present?

1. The city has grown a lot *since* 1970.
2. The Romans built that monumental building nearly 2,000 years *ago*.
3. The new part of the city has changed a lot *recently*.
4. The Romans founded the city of Ogrium *in* 22 AD.
5. The Romans occupied it *for* nearly four hundred years.
6. Ogland has been an independent country *for* over six hundred years.

E
Which tense do we use with the expressions below? Past simple, present perfect, or both?

since / in 22 AD / ago / recently / for

What is the difference in meaning between the two uses of *for*? What is the difference between *for* and *since*?

F
In groups, talk about changes in your own city, town or village. Prepare ten sentences; five using the past simple and five using the present perfect.
Include expressions like those in exercise E.
Read your sentences out to the class and see if they agree.

G
In groups, look at the network. One student says a word and the next makes a sentence with that word. If the sentence is correct, he/she gets a point.

Example: A: for
B: I've lived here *for* six years.
Correct: one point
B: in
C: I've bought a BMX bike *in* 1990.
Wrong: no points

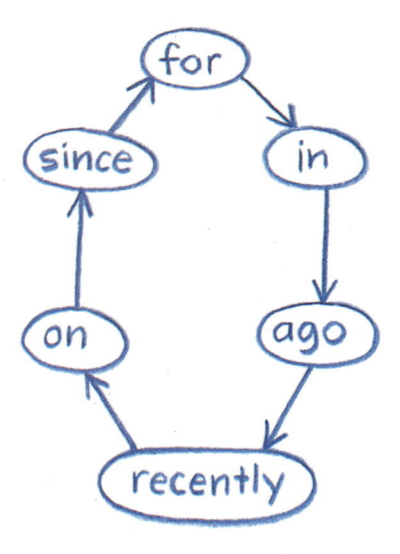

(Network diagram with words: for, since, in, on, ago, recently)

33

14 Revision

Listening

A

In two teams, listen to the questions and try to answer them.

Speaking

B

In groups, imagine it is the year 2050. Take turns to talk about your childhood memories. Talk about school, hobbies, family, music, sport, holidays, etc.

Example: A: I remember I used to get the bus to school.
B: I used to walk to school.
C: I didn't use to like school.
D: Mmm, I used to hate maths.

C

In pairs, tell your partner you have done something unusual. Your partner tells you he/she did it before you! Student A looks at number 3 on page 108, Student B looks at number 3 on page 110.

Example: A: I've read all of Shakespeare's plays.
B: Me too. I read them two years ago!

Language revision

D

Rewrite each sentence using the correct form of *used to*.

Example: 1 I didn't *use to* like cheese.

1 I didn't like cheese when I was young. Now I love it!
2 I lived in a small village before I came to the city.
3 She studied hard last year, but now she goes out every night.
4 Many years ago, that man was very poor.
5 Where did you go on holiday when you were young?

E

Match the two parts of each sentence and put the verbs in the correct tense, past simple or present perfect.

1 Simon Bolivar (die) a) over 1000 years ago.
2 The Vikings (live) b) in 1830.
3 English (become) very important c) for two years.
4 France (be) a Republic d) recently.
5 I (study) English e) since 1789.

Learner training

F LEARN TO LEARN

Check the meaning of the verbs below in the mini-dictionary. Then complete the sentences. Remember to put the verbs in the correct tense.

get around / try out / get up / come across

1 You can . . . . . Venice on a gondola.
2 She used to . . . . . at half past five.
3 We walked around Paris and . . . . . a lovely restaurant.
4 They hurried home to . . . . . their new video game.

G LEARN TO LEARN

Vocabulary questionnaire. Answer these questions honestly!

☐ How many new words have you written down from this module?
☐ Compare this number with another student.
☐ Do you mark words N (noun), V (verb), ADJ (adjective), etc.?
☐ Do you always mark the stress?
☐ Do you give a translation in your own language?
☐ Do you put the words in a key sentence?

34

Writing

H

Write about the life of Bob Marley.

1945	is born in Jamaica
1960	makes first record – forms his group, The Wailers
1966	goes to the USA – quickly has to return to Jamaica to do military service
1968	reggae music becomes more popular – Marley sings songs about freedom, politics, love and religion – everybody can understand his message
1976	somebody tries to kill Marley before a concert
1978–80	plays important concerts for Peace in Jamaica and Zimbabwe
1981	dies of cancer

Stage 1 Read the key facts and put the verbs in the past tense. Check irregular verbs in the list at the back of the book.

Stage 2 Look at lesson 10, exercise E and think about where you can put some of these words to join the key facts.

Stage 3 Divide the information into three parts – early life; what made him famous; the last years.

Stage 4 Write a short biography in three paragraphs.

I

Now do the Module check on page 107.

Language check

PAST SIMPLE

Regular verbs
The Vikings **sailed** in wooden boats.
They **didn't sail** to Australia.
Did the Vikings **sail** to America?

Irregular verbs
Amy Johnson **flew** to Australia.
She **didn't fly** round the world.
Did she **fly** back home?

Obligation
(Affirmative)
Bolivar **had to** escape to Jamaica.

Ability
I **could** swim when I was five, but I **couldn't** speak English.
Could you read before you went to school?

USED TO

They **used to** pay children very little.
There **didn't use to** be a cinema in my town.
Did you **use to** play with dolls?

PAST SIMPLE OR PRESENT PERFECT?

The Aztecs **built** an empire **in the 15th century**.
Tenochtitlan **was** bigger than any city in Europe **450 years ago**.
The Ancient Romans **dominated** Europe **for over 400 years**.

My town **has changed** a lot **since 1980**.
Tourism **has increased** in the **last 20 years**.
We **have had** a lot of homework **recently**.
I **have lived** in Athens **for five years**.

MODULE 3
FANTASY

15 World of horror

A
Match the pictures with the words below.

werewolf / vampire / rats / giant spider / ghost / monster

Which of the things are real?

B
Put the creatures in order of how frightening they are.

Example: 1 vampires
2 giant spiders

C
Copy the table. Then listen to the interview and complete it.

	Fears now	Fears when younger
George	rats	
Linda		

Fact or fantasy?

Viking soldiers called Beserkers used to look like werewolves. They wore wolf skins and had long hair and beards to frighten their enemies.

(Answer on page 122)

Pronunciation

D 🎧
Copy the sentences below. Then listen and mark the main stress in the sentences.

Example: 1 What **things** are you **afraid** of?

1 What things are you afraid of?
2 Well, I don't like rats at all.
3 I think they're really horrible things.
4 I saw a huge rat crossing the street.
5 Well, I used to be afraid of ghosts.
6 I used to think there was a ghost in the garden.

E
In groups, find out what the others are afraid of.

Example: A: How do you feel about rats?
B: Very frightened!
C: A bit nervous.
D: Relaxed . . . they don't frighten me.

What thing is the group most afraid of?

F
In groups, find out what the others used to be afraid of.

Example: A: Did you use to be afraid of ghosts?
B: Yes, I did. / No, I didn't.

G
Look at the two mixed-up stories. Which of the creatures from exercise A is each one about? Read them again and list which sentences are from each story. Do you think the stories are true?

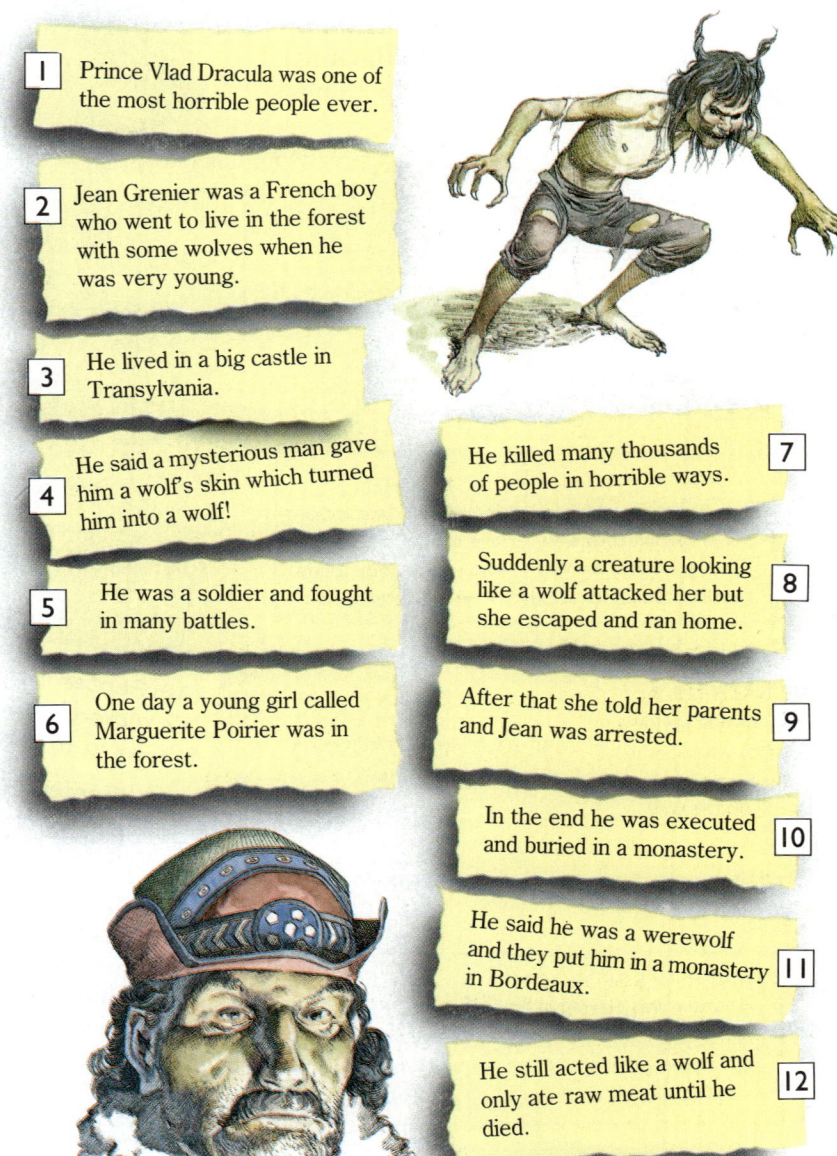

1 Prince Vlad Dracula was one of the most horrible people ever.

2 Jean Grenier was a French boy who went to live in the forest with some wolves when he was very young.

3 He lived in a big castle in Transylvania.

4 He said a mysterious man gave him a wolf's skin which turned him into a wolf!

5 He was a soldier and fought in many battles.

6 One day a young girl called Marguerite Poirier was in the forest.

7 He killed many thousands of people in horrible ways.

8 Suddenly a creature looking like a wolf attacked her but she escaped and ran home.

9 After that she told her parents and Jean was arrested.

10 In the end he was executed and buried in a monastery.

11 He said he was a werewolf and they put him in a monastery in Bordeaux.

12 He still acted like a wolf and only ate raw meat until he died.

H
Look at the story of Jean Grenier again and list the linking words.

Example: . . . he went to live in the forest *when* he was young.

37

16 The haunted house

A
Do you think that ghosts exist? Have you ever been to a haunted place?

B
Look at the diagram. Which of the things that happened do you think was the most frightening? Why do you think the things happened?

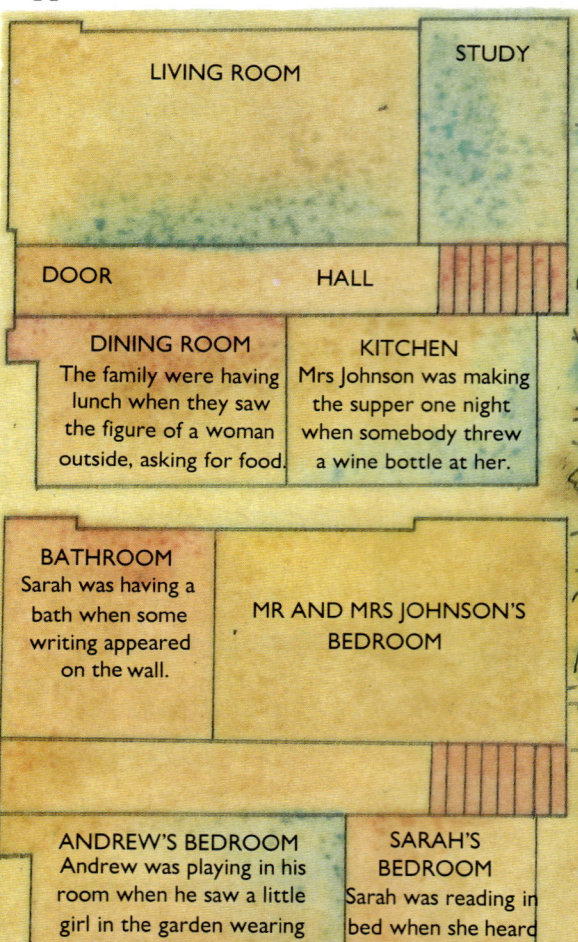

LIVING ROOM

STUDY

DOOR

HALL

DINING ROOM
The family were having lunch when they saw the figure of a woman outside, asking for food.

KITCHEN
Mrs Johnson was making the supper one night when somebody threw a wine bottle at her.

BATHROOM
Sarah was having a bath when some writing appeared on the wall.

MR AND MRS JOHNSON'S BEDROOM

ANDREW'S BEDROOM
Andrew was playing in his room when he saw a little girl in the garden wearing old-fashioned clothes.

SARAH'S BEDROOM
Sarah was reading in bed when she heard terrible screams.

C
Read the diary and find out the cause of the hauntings. Then use the diagram to complete the diary.

Example: 1 = playing

19th September
We moved into our new house today. It's got a fantastic garden.

22nd September
Somebody at school said our new house is haunted. I don't believe in ghosts!

6th October
Andrew was 1___ in his room this afternoon when he saw a little girl in the garden. The girl was 2___ old-fashioned clothes. I think Andrew is seeing things!

31st October
Halloween! I was 3___ a bath tonight when some writing suddenly appeared on the wall. It said 'GET OUT'. I looked at the writing and it was in blood! I am getting scared!

18th November
We were in the dining room and we were 4___ lunch, when we saw the figure of a woman outside. She was 5___ for food and looking at our plates. This is not funny any more!

Language focus:
PAST CONTINUOUS / PAST SIMPLE

D
Look at these sentences from the diary. Put them in order of when they happened.

a) I looked at the writing.
b) I was having a bath.
c) Writing suddenly appeared on the wall.

Which tense is used to describe:

- an activity (what I was doing)?
- an action (what happened)?
- a reaction (what happened after that)?

5th December
Mum was 6 ___ supper in the kitchen when somebody threw a wine bottle at her. She says there was nobody else in the kitchen. She wants to leave the house.

25th December
Last night was horrible! It was very late and I couldn't sleep. I was 7 ___ in bed when I heard terrible screams and all the windows smashed. Somehow we all got out of the house. Outside everything was quiet. We are never going into that house again and we have decided to sell it.

6th January
I went to the local library today. I found out that the house had been the old poorhouse. It closed in 1892, after the director had gone mad and murdered several of the poor people. The murders happened on the 24th of December!!!

E
Copy and complete these tables.

PAST CONTINUOUS

Affirmative

I/He/She/It	.....	having	lunch.
You/We/They	.....	.....	a book.

Negative

I/He/She/It	.....	not	having a shower.
You/We/They	.....		

Questions

What	.....	I/he/she/it	doing?
	.....	you/we/they	

F
Write five negative sentences about the story.

Example: Sarah wasn't sleeping when she heard the screams.

G
Imagine that you lived in the haunted house. Invent five things that happened when you were there.

Example: I was listening to music in my room when I saw a horrible face at the window.

H
In pairs, interview your partner, like this:

Action   A: What happened?
Activity   A: What were you doing when it happened?
Reaction   A: What did you do?

17 Fantastic films

Gremlins

Frankenstein

Twenty thousand leagues under the sea

A
In pairs, find out which of the films your partner has seen.

Example: A: Have you seen *Gremlins*?
B: Yes, I have.
A: Did you like it?
B: Yes, it was great.

B
Listen to the two dialogues. Answer these questions.

1 What film did Sue and Dave go and see?
2 When did Kate and Richard go to the cinema?
3 What film did they decide to see?
4 When and where did they arrange to meet?

C
Listen to the first dialogue again and complete it.

SUE: I feel like going out this afternoon. [1] . . . . . we go to the cinema?
DAVE: There's nothing on at the moment.
SUE: Yes, there is. [2] . . . . . go and see *Gremlins*? It's a brilliant film. I really want to see it again.
DAVE: No, [3] . . . . . staying in and watching the football on television?
SUE: Oh no! Come on! [4] . . . . . go and see the film!
DAVE: OK, you win. But I'd rather watch the football.

Pronunciation

D
Listen to the six sentences. Write down the words you hear.

Example: 1 Shall we go to the cinema?

E
Listen again. Which words in the sentences become joined:

Example: 1 Shall we . . .

Listen to the sentences again and repeat them quickly.

40

Batman

Alien

E.T.

F
Plan your diary for next week. Include three things that you often do.

	afternoon	evening
Monday		
Tuesday		
Wednesday	swimming lesson 4 pm	
Thursday		
Friday		judo class
Saturday	go skateboarding in park	
Sunday		

G
In groups, invite people to go with you to see a film.

Example: A: Would you like to come and see *Alien* on Wednesday afternoon?
B: I'm sorry, I'm busy. I'm going swimming.
A: Let's go and see *E.T.* on Wednesday evening.
B: OK, that's a good idea. What time shall we meet?
A: How about meeting at eight o'clock outside the cinema?

Write down the films you arrange to see in your diary, like this:

Alien 6pm with Sandra

Fact or fantasy?

Bela Lugosi, the most famous Dracula of the cinema, was born in Romania, traditional home of the vampire.

(Answer on page 122)

18 The rescue

1. A British ship was sailing in the Arctic Ocean in the 1860s, when something very strange happened. A sailor called Robert Bruce went to the captain's cabin and saw a stranger writing in the captain's logbook. Bruce was terrified, because no one had boarded the ship since they left Liverpool.

2. When Bruce told the captain, they looked at the logbook and saw that someone had written 'Go northwest'. The captain suspected a joke and decided to find out who had done it. He told all the crew to write 'Go northwest', to test their handwriting. Not one of them had the same handwriting.

3. Robert Bruce was sure that he had seen the man and the captain decided to go northwest. They discovered a ship which had got stuck in the ice. When they got to the ship, the survivors had almost given up hope. Bruce was shocked, because he had seen one of the sailors before – in the captain's cabin, writing in the logbook.

4. The captain tested the man's writing and it was the same as the mysterious original. The stranger could not remember writing the message, but said that he had fallen into a deep sleep at about that time. He had dreamed that he was on a ship that was coming to save them.

A
Have you ever dreamed about something that really happened later? Have you ever dreamed that you left your body?

B
Match the pictures with the correct paragraph.

Language focus: PAST PERFECT

C
Look at these pairs of sentences. Which event happened first, a) or b)?

1. a) Bruce was terrified.
   b) No-one had boarded the ship since Liverpool.
2. a) They looked at the logbook.
   b) Someone had written 'Go northwest.'
3. a) They got to the ship.
   b) The survivors had almost given up hope.
4. a) Bruce was shocked.
   b) He had seen the man before.

What is the past perfect tense used for?

D
Copy and complete the tables.

	Subject	Auxiliary	Participle	Object
Affirmative	I / You / He / She / We / They	.....	.....	the man before.
Negative		..... not	.....	'Go northwest'.

	Auxiliary	Subject	Participle	Object
Question	.....	I / you / he / she / we / they	.....	hope?

Find other examples of the past perfect in the story.

E
Use the notes below to write about what had happened before the rescue.

Example: 1 The ship had left Liverpool.

1 ship / leave / Liverpool
2 Bruce / see / stranger
3 stranger / write / in / logbook
4 Captain / not / believe / Bruce
5 he / test / crew's / handwriting
6 he / decide / to go / northwest

F
In groups, play the backward story game. This is the ending to the story:

We ran along the street and arrived back home. We were very frightened.

You have to find a beginning! In groups, write sentences, like this:

Before that: . . . we had escaped from a ghost.
    . . . the ghost had been an old man with strange eyes.
    . . . we had seen the ghost in the garden of a deserted house.

19 Monsters

A
Look at the drawings of the three monsters. Which of them do you think is the most dangerous? Now read the descriptions and decide.

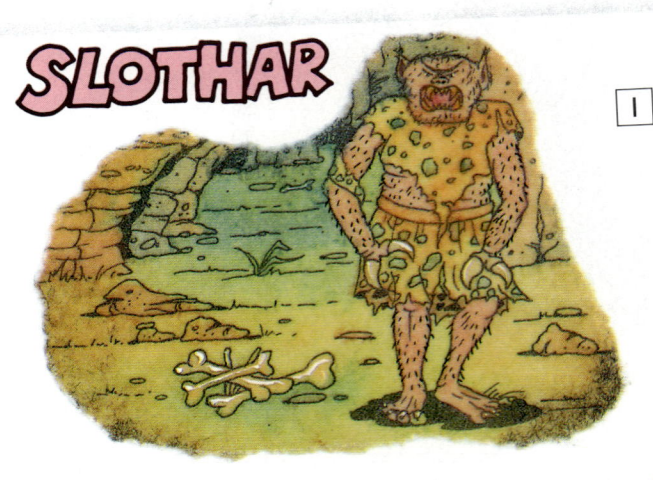

SLOTHAR

1. **The Slothar** is an enormous creature, nearly three metres tall. It has a sinister square head, covered with thin brown hair. Its eyes are small, but it has a large mouth with horrible pointed yellow teeth. At the end of its long arms there are two sharp claws to kill its victims with. It wears old animal skins to keep it warm in the caves. Usually it moves very slowly and sleeps a lot, but when it is hungry it can run fast. The Slothar is extremely dangerous because it eats all living things, including humans!

VENORA

2. **Venora**, the snakewoman is graceful and elegant. She has a beautiful pattern of bright red and blue on her skin. Her legs and arms are long and delicate and she has a small head, the head of a snake. There are two sinister small green eyes on the sides of her head and a long pink tongue slides in and out of her mouth. Venora bites her victims with her two sharp fangs and they quickly become unconscious. Then she drinks their blood!

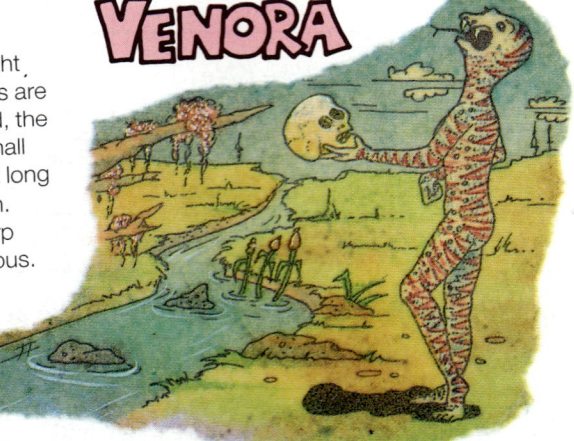

HYPNOTH

3. **The Hypnoth** does not look very dangerous. He is like a small old man, not quite a metre tall and with very thin legs and arms. The really strange thing about him is his head and in particular his eyes. His head is too big for his body and he has got two enormous bright blue eyes. He usually wears elegant old-fashioned clothes and he looks very friendly. But if you look into his eyes, he will hypnotise you and you will be in his power. You will become part of his zoological collection!

B
Copy and complete the table with adjectives from the text.

Monster	General	Size/Shape	Colour	Object
Slothar	sinister –	square		head hair teeth
Venora	–			eyes tongue
Hypnoth	–			eyes

C
Look at the different stages for writing a description. In which order did the writer do each one?

A
The Slothar is an enormous creature, nearly three metres tall. It has got a sinister square head, covered with thin brown hair. Its eyes are small, but it has got a large mouth with horrible pointed yellow teeth. At the end of its long arms there are two sharp claws to kill its victims with. It wears old animal skins to keep it warm in the caves. Usually it moves very slowly and it sleeps a lot, but when it is hungry it can run fast. The Slothar is extremely dangerous because it eats all living things, including humans!

B
The Slothar is ~~a big~~ an enormous creature, nearly ~~two and a half~~ three metres tall. It has got a sinister square head, covered with ~~thick~~ thin brown hair. Its eyes are small, ~~and~~ but it has got a large mouth with horrible pointed yellow teeth. At the end of ~~it's~~ its long arms there are two sharp claws to kill its victims with. It wears old animal skins to keep it warm in the caves. Usually it moves very slowly and it sleeps a lot, but when it is hungry it can ~~move~~ run very fast. The Slothar is extremely dangerous because it eats all living things, including humans!

C (plan)
- SIZE: big
- FACE: pointed teeth, small eyes
- HAIR: thick/brown
- BODY: long arms, ~~powerful~~
- BEHAVIOUR: sleeps a lot, wears animal skins, moves slowly/can run fast
- MONSTER

D
Write a description of your own monster.

Stage 1 Do a plan (like C). Include information about: face/hair/body/size/behaviour.

Stage 2 Use the plan to write a rough description.

Stage 3 Check your description. Correct mistakes and make changes.

Stage 4 Write out your final description.

E
In groups, describe your monster. Others in the group try to draw your monster. When you have finished, look at the drawings and decide which is the best.

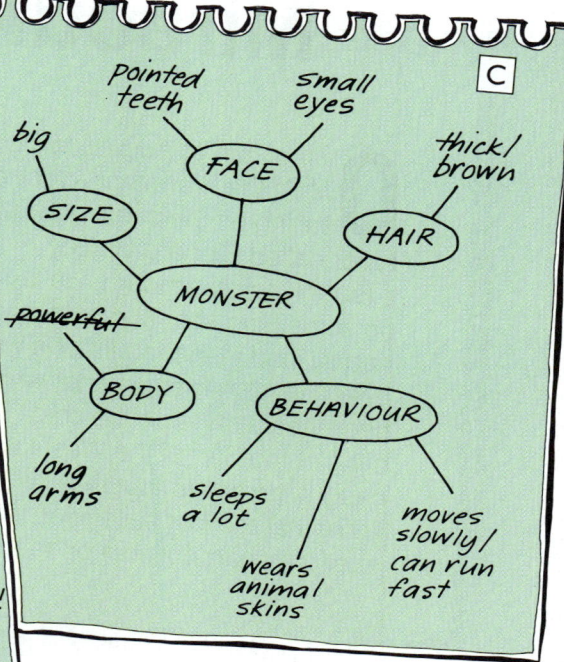

20 Believe it or not?

AMAZING BUT TRUE

Miraculous Escape

On the 26th of August 1871, while the Star of the West was sailing off the coast of Brazil, a sailor called Richard Bartley suddenly fell overboard. He landed on something soft. Miraculously he had landed in the mouth of a whale over thirty-five metres long, which had been alongside the ship. The crew of the Star of the West later caught the whale, but they did not know that the lost sailor was in it. After they had pulled it on to the deck and cut it up, they saw a movement inside the stomach. When they opened it they found Bartley lying inside, unconscious. He had spent over six hours in the stomach of this creature, but he survived and in the end he recovered completely. However, while he was lying in the beast's stomach the acids in it had changed the colour of his skin and it remained yellow for the rest of his life.

A

Have you ever heard a story you thought was false, but later you found out was true? Tell your partner.

B

Listen to the story of James Bartley. Do you believe the story? Why? Why not?

C

Read the article on the left. Then listen to the story again. There are seven factual mistakes in the article. What are they?

Example: 1 The ship was called the 'Star of the *East*', not 'Star of the West'.

Fact or fantasy?

Baron Munchausen was a famous German traveller. Once, he was travelling in Poland in the winter. He tied his horse to a post and went to sleep on the snow. When he woke up the snow had gone and his horse was tied to the top of a church tower.

(Answer on page 122)

Language focus: NARRATIVE – PAST TENSES

D

Read the article again and find examples of these three tenses:

- Past perfect • Past simple • Past continuous

Example: Miraculously he *had landed* in the mouth of a whale . . .
    = Past perfect

Which tense is used:

a) to describe an action that happened in the past?
b) to describe something that happened before something else?
c) to describe an activity in the past?

E

Imagine you are Bartley. Retell the story. Copy and complete the sentences below.

While I . . . . . I suddenly . . . . .
I realised that I . . . . .
After ten minutes I . . . . .
When I woke up I . . . . .
In the end I . . . . . but my skin . . . . .

F

Think of a real situation (or invent one) in which you were in danger but you escaped. Write notes about the things below.

Example: 1 On a farm when I was five years old.

1 When and where did it happen?
2 What were you doing when it happened? (playing near a pond)
3 What happened to you? (fell into pond – couldn't swim)
4 How did you escape? (farmer heard me fall in *and* pulled me out)
5 How did you feel afterwards? (frightened/wet – never played near pond again)

G

In groups, tell your story and listen to the others'. Decide if the other stories are true or not. Choose the best story to tell the whole class.

21 Revision

Listening

A 🔲

Listen to the descriptions. Who or what are they describing?

Speaking

B 💬

Copy this form.

Ghost report   GHOST HUNTERS

Date _10/03/68_
Reporter _Mrs O'Brien_
Time _9.00 p.m._
Place _Killakee House, Ireland_
Description _A black figure and a black cat_
Activity _standing in the garden/sitting in the hall_

Then invent a ghost and complete the form.

C 💬

In pairs, find out about the ghost your partner saw.

Example: When did you see the ghost?
Where did you see it?
What was it doing?

Language revision

D

Read part of the story of *The Black Cat of Killakee*. Do you believe it? Put the verbs in brackets into the past continuous, the past simple or the past perfect.

Killakee House is a large old house near Dublin in Ireland. Before Mrs O'Brien (move) [1] ..... into it in 1968 the house (be) [2] ..... the scene of a lot of violence. The villagers (tell) [3] ..... her that because of the things that (happen) [4] ..... there the house was haunted.

One night in March 1968 Mrs O'Brien was with some friends in the house. They (paint) [5] ..... the hall of the house, when the door (open) [6] ..... They (see) [7] ..... a figure outside. It (wear) [8] ..... black clothes and (stand) [9] ..... in the garden, but she (cannot) [10] ..... see the face.

E

Read the second part of the story. Find mistakes for each of these things and mark them, like this:

S = spelling   G = grammar
Pr = prepositions

Then try to correct the mistakes.

Example: mysteri^o us

The mysterius figure said at her: 'Leave this door open!' When Mrs O'Brien heard that, she closed the front door and ran towards the kitchen door. Before she have got there she looked back. The door was open and an enormous black cat had come in the hall and was sit there looking to her with horible large red eyes.

Learner training

F
Look at the mistakes in exercise E again and grade them, like this:

★★★★★ = a really horrible mistake
★★★ = a bad mistake
★ = not very bad

Writing

G
Write a horror story about one of these things.

vampires / ghosts / werewolves / monsters

Stage 1 Choose the subject and write down ten words about it.
Stage 2 Use your rough notes to plan four paragraphs, like this:
  1 *Situation:*
    where you were
    what you were doing
    what time it was
  2 *What happened:*
    what you saw or heard
    a description
  3 *Reaction:*
    what you did
    (*Example:* try to run away)
  4 *Conclusions:*
    what happened in the end
Stage 3 Write a first draft. Try to use some of these linking words:
  after / before / when / while / suddenly / immediately / later / in the end
Stage 4 Give your story to your partner to look for mistakes (S / G / Pr).
Stage 5 Write a final version of the story.

H
Look at the Module check on page 107.

Language check

NARRATIVE TENSES
PAST CONTINUOUS

Affirmative
I **was reading** in bed (when I heard horrible screams).
We **were having** lunch (when we saw the figure of a woman).

Negative
She **was not listening** (when Sarah spoke).

Questions
What **were you doing** (when you saw the face)?

PAST PERFECT

Affirmative
Somebody **had written** 'Go northwest'.
He **had seen** the man before.

Negative
The sailors **had not written** in the logbook.

Questions
Had Bruce seen the man before?

LINKING

While he was working on deck he fell overboard.
After they had cut it up they pulled it on deck.
When they opened it they found Bartley inside.
When he had recovered he had white skin.

MODULE 4 NATURE

22 The seasons

Nature Watch

1. In which month of the year does it begin to get warmer?
2. When do leaves start growing on the trees?
3. Do any birds migrate to your area? If so, when do they arrive?
4. When do animals and birds start breeding where you live?
5. In which months do plants in local parks and gardens have lots of flowers?
6. How long is the summer?
7. When do the leaves start to fall?
8. Are there any animals in your country that hibernate in the winter?
9. In which month does it begin to get colder?
10. What is the weather like in the winter?

A
In pairs, read the questionnaire and agree on the answers.

B
In groups, discuss your answers. Report the group answers to the rest of the class.

Example: 1 It begins to get warmer in March.

C
Listen to Lucy. Answer the questions below.

1 Where did she live for two years?
2 What is the weather like there in the summer?
3 How often does it rain?
4 How long is the desert spring?

D
Listen again and order the sentences below describing spring in the Mojave desert.

a) Finally, after a few weeks, the plants die and it gets hotter.
b) After a few days the desert is full of flowers.
c) Then all the plants start growing.
d) First it rains a lot.
e) Lots of insects and small animals come out to breed.

Pronunciation

E
Listen to the different ways you can pronounce the letter 'o'.

Group 1	Group 2	Group 3	Group 4	Group 5
/ɒ/ not	/ʌ/ some	/əʊ/ so	/uː/ too	/ɔː/ normal

Which group do these words belong to?

you / two / lots / got / enormous / know / hot / does / month / grow / sorts / covered / frogs / come / dormant / goes

Example: you = Group 4

F
Listen to this description and write it down.

Example: Four young people who . . .

When you have finished see how many words you can find with the letter 'o' in them.

Nature project

G
Write about a season where you live.

Stage 1 Look at your answers for exercise A. Write notes about weather and about changes in plants and animals.

Stage 2 Use your notes to write a short paragraph.

Keep this paragraph for the project in Lesson 28.

Did you know?

The African lungfish is a small fish that lives in desert areas. It can live underground for nine years, breathing with its lungs. When it rains it comes out and lives like a fish!

51

23 Wonders of nature

A
Match the adjectives with the four animals in the photos.

deadly / beautiful / delicate / strange / curious / sinister / thin / dangerous

Example: 1 = curious / thin

B
Read the texts and choose one of these titles for each text:

- Lord of darkness
- Nature's helicopter
- Master of disguise
- Deadly assassin

C
Look at the note network for a stick insect. Complete note networks like this for the other three animals.

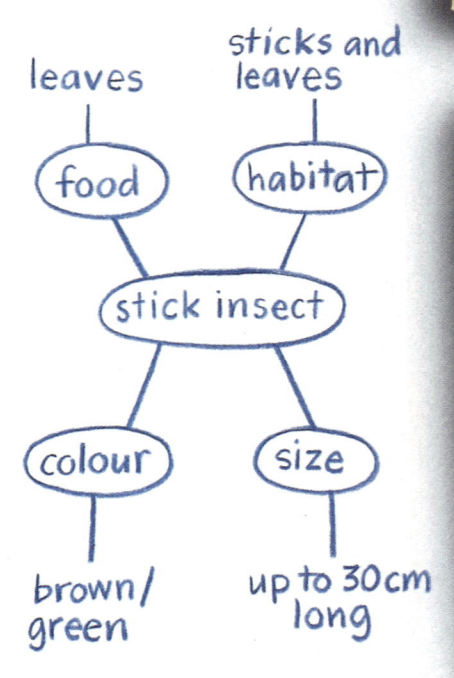

Spot the insect!

The best experts at disguise in nature are stick and leaf insects. Their bodies look just like the sticks and leaves where they live and they can stay for hours without moving. These curious insects are incredibly thin, though the biggest can be up to thirty centimetres long. Some oriental stick insects make popular pets and are easy to feed with leaves. The most interesting stick insects can even change colour, becoming a paler brown by day and darker by night.

A group of horror film extras.

The vampire bat is the only dangerous one among the 951 different species of bat. It is one of the strangest and most sinister creatures in the world. The common vampire bat is brown and is six to nine centimetres long. It lives near rivers and prefers hunting on the darkest nights, when there is no moon,

The terrible smile of the Great White.

The shark has always had a bad reputation and the Great White (the star of the film *Jaws*), has the worst of all. It is the most dangerous shark that exists and perhaps the deadliest assassin of the animal kingdom, killing large animals like dolphins. It likes hunting in shallow water near beaches and has killed many people. With its impressive teeth it can even bite through metal cables and boats! The biggest white sharks are up to six metres long and weigh up to 1800 kilos, with a large stomach big enough to hold a complete human body.

Note network:
- leaves → food
- sticks and leaves → habitat
- stick insect
- colour → brown/green
- size → up to 30cm long

attacking cows, horses, pigs and sometimes human beings. It has twenty-two teeth and it uses the two biggest and sharpest of these to make a cut in its victim. The vampire bat then drinks the blood, just like Dracula!

Feeding from a flower in Mexico.

Perhaps the most beautiful and delicate bird in the world is the hummingbird. Hummingbirds are tiny, brightly coloured creatures, which live in forests and feed from the nectar of flowers. The smallest of all is the bee hummingbird, which only weighs two grams and has the smallest nest in the bird world, about the size of a grape. Not only can hummingbirds fly like other birds, but they can hover in the air just like helicopters, moving their wings up to 200 times per second.

Language focus: SUPERLATIVES

D
Use the texts to copy and complete the tables.

Short adjectives

	Comparative	Superlative
thin	thinner	the thinnest
big		
small		
deadly		

Irregular adjectives

	Comparative	Superlative
good	better	best
bad		

Long adjectives

	Comparative	Superlative
dangerous	more dangerous	the most/least dangerous
sinister		
interesting		

Add other adjectives from the texts to your tables.

E
Use the information below to write five questions about the animals.

Example: What is the biggest animal in the world?

1 **Size:**   *maximum:* blue whale (33m long / weight 130 tonnes)
             minimum: pygmy shrew (3.8cm long)
2 **Height:** *maximum:* Masai giraffe (5.87m)
3 **Speed:** *maximum:* cheetah (115kph)
             minimum: sloth (2kph)

F
In pairs, close your books and ask your partner your questions. Can you remember the answers?

Example: A: What is the biggest animal in the world?
          B: The blue whale. It is . . .

53

24 Your planet needs you!

A

In pairs, look at the photos and match them with the questions below. Then try to answer the questions.

1 What everyday objects can we recycle?
2 What causes air pollution and acid rain?
3 Which of the world's seas are the most polluted?
4 What is happening to the world's rain forests?
5 What destroys the ozone layer?
6 What is happening to the world's climate?

B
Check your answers by reading this leaflet:

Friends of the Earth is fighting on these issues:

RECYCLING
We can still do more to recycle glass, paper, cans and plastic.

AIR POLLUTION
Pollution from factories and cars poisons the air we breathe and causes acid rain, which kills our trees.

WATER POLLUTION
Many of our seas, like the North Sea and the Mediterranean, are full of chemicals and sewage.

SAVING THE RAINFOREST
In Brazil's rainforests an area roughly the size of England and Wales is destroyed every year.

THE OZONE LAYER
Chemicals like the CFCs found in fridges are damaging the ozone layer.

THE GREENHOUSE EFFECT
The world's temperature is going up and the climate is changing.

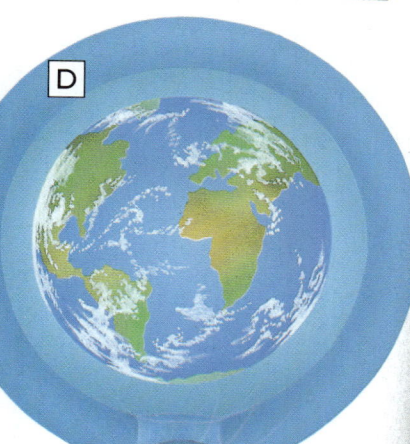

C

Listen to the interview with Alison. Which of the problems in the leaflet does Alison mention?

Example: the rainforests

D

Listen again. Complete the questionnaire for Alison.

▶▶▶▶ How green are you? ◀◀◀◀

1 What do you do to recycle things?
   Collect newspapers/use recycled paper

2 What do you do to save energy?
   ....

3 What do you do to help animals and wildlife?
   ....

4 Are you and your family green shoppers?
   ....

E

In groups, use the questionnaire to find out who is the 'greenest' person in your group.

Nature project

F

Make a list of practical ways that we can help the planet. Think about some of the things below.

paper / electricity / tins / bottles / petrol / animals / birds / food / shopping / gardens / pets / trees / rivers / the sea

Example: We should always write on both sides of the paper, to save paper. We shouldn't leave lights on and waste electricity.

Keep this list for the project in Lesson 28.

Did you know?

The cleanest form of transport is the bicycle. The dirtiest is the private car.

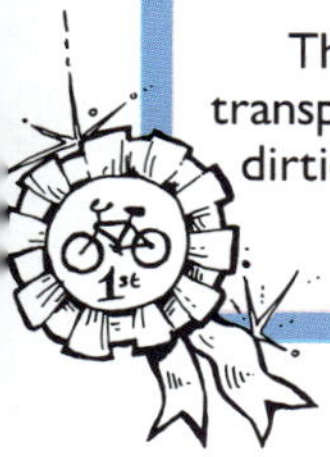

25 Takuana island

A [LEARN TO LEARN]

Which of these things do you listen to in English?

- People who speak English as a second language
- My partner in class
- Pop songs in English
- The cassette in class
- People from the USA
- Films on video
- My teacher
- British people

Grade the listening activities, like this:

★★★★★	= I understand nearly everything.
★★★	= I get the general idea.
★	= I understand a few words.

B [LEARN TO LEARN]

When you listen to a cassette in class, which of these things do you think are good or bad?

1. Before I listen, I try to predict what it will be about.
2. When I am not sure about the questions I ask the teacher.
3. While listening I use my dictionary.
4. I try to translate every word the first time I hear something.
5. When it is difficult and I only understand a few words I stop listening.
6. I try to listen for important words.

C

Look at the pictures before you listen to a radio programme about Takuana. What subjects do you think the programme will mention? Listen and check your answers.

- Birds and animals
- New hospitals and schools
- Factories and mines
- Destruction of rain forests
- Famous people from Takuana
- Sport
- Takuana history
- Pollution
- Takuana cooking
- The Takuana language
- Traditional houses

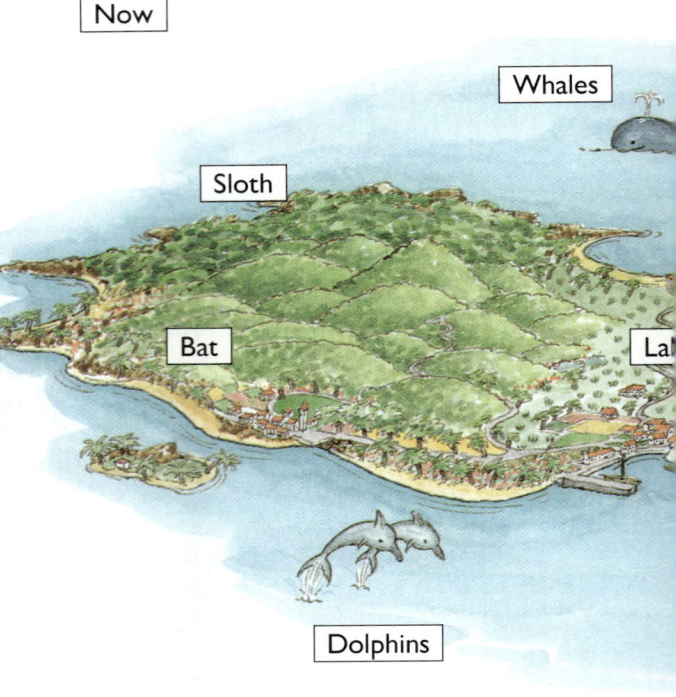

56

Language focus: CONDITIONAL SENTENCES (1)

D
Listen again. Match the two parts of the sentences.

1 If they build an airport in the marshes,
2 What will happen to the island
3 If they build a port,
4 If thousands of people come to the island,
5 If they destroy the rainforest,

a) the climate will change.
b) they will pollute the sea.
c) many species of birds will disappear.
d) if they do that?
e) the Taku language will disappear.

E
Look at the conditional sentences in exercise D again. Which tenses are used? Copy and complete the chart.

Condition	Consequence
If they build a port, If + ... tense	they will pollute the sea. + ... tense

Now use the maps to write four more conditional sentences about the plans for the island.

F
In groups, read out your sentences and discuss the advantages (+) and disadvantages (−) of the plan.

Example: A: (−) If they destroy the forest, the Takuana hummingbird will disappear.
B: (+) Yes, but if they build factories the people will have jobs.

Pronunciation

G
Listen to six sentences. Write down the key words.

Example: 1 If / destroy / rainforest / climate / change

57

26 Speak out!

National Tin Corporation,
10 Stamford Road,
London EC2

May 2nd

Dear Sir/Madam,

[1] I would like to explain to your readers the effects of the new development plans on Takuana. Many people are worried about them, because a lot of so-called 'green' groups are giving out false information.

[2] There will be important changes in the island. However, these will be good for the people. Although the island is pretty, it is one of the poorest places in the world. If we start mining and processing the tin there will be lots of jobs for the people of Takuana. They will have good hospitals, schools, roads and sports facilities. There will be lots of new, modern houses and flats for them and better communications with the new international airport.

[3] It is true that there will be some pollution, but much less than the 'greens' say there will. Although there will be mines and factories, these will be modern and will have strict pollution controls. To reduce air pollution there will be a nuclear power station, which will provide electricity. There will be less rainforest, but we will be able to conserve all the rare animals in Nature reserves.

[4] In my opinion the new development will bring progress and prosperity to the island. However, I will be in Taku City next month to attend the public meeting and I look forward to discussing the plan with the people of Takuana then.

Yours faithfully,

Phei Chang

Phei Chang (chief executive)

A

Read the letter to the *Taku Herald* newspaper.

1. Is the letter in favour of the development plan or against it?
2. List five advantages of the plan.
3. Match these subjects with the correct paragraphs:
   - advantages of the plan
   - pollution and conservation
   - reasons for writing letter
   - public meeting

B
What do the words below refer to in the letter?

Example: them (line 2) = the development plans

them (line 2) / these (line 5) / it (line 6) / they (line 8) / them (line 10) / these (line 14) / then (line 21)

C
Look at these sentences from the letter.

There will be important changes in the island. *However*, these will be good for the people.
Although the island is pretty, it is one of the poorest places in the world.
There will be some pollution, *but* much less than the 'greens' say there will.

Write three more sentences about the plans using the words in *italics*.

D
Form into these groups:

- students from Takuana
- ecological groups
- local Taku business people
- local farmers
- representatives of foreign businesses

Decide if you are for or against the plan. List your reasons, like this:

For: (+) If they build the airport, we will have better communications.
Against: (−) If they build the factories and mines, we will lose our farms.

You can also think of an alternative plan, like this:

If we only build hotels, we will be richer but we won't destroy the island.

E
One person from each group reports to the class. Then the class votes to accept or reject the plan.

Nature project

F
Write a letter about an ecological problem in your area, for example, traffic.

Stage 1 Choose the problem and write down ten words about it.
Stage 2 Use the rough notes to plan paragraphs:
  1 reasons for writing
  2 information about problem (*Example*: traffic: causes traffic jams, air pollution, etc.)
  3 what we should do about the problem (more public transport, etc.)
Stage 3 Look at the letter in exercise A to find out where to put the address / how to begin / how to finish.
Stage 4 Use your notes to write the letter.

Keep this letter for your project in Lesson 28.

Did you know?

Dolphins like swimming near to tuna in the ocean. In the last few years, more than seven million dolphins have died in fishing nets.

27 Operation Tiger

A
Read about Operation Tiger and answer the questions.

1 Why did the numbers of tigers in India go down?
2 When did the campaign start?
3 How many reserves did they create?
4 What happened to the people from the reserves?
5 How many tigers are there now in India?

B
Read the text again. Write notes about the things below.

Example: Species of animals: thousands lost / many close to extinction

- species of animals
- tiger hunters
- number of tigers
- special tiger reserves
- the people from the reserves
- the tigers now

Did you know?
The best-known extinct creature is the dodo, which disappeared in 1681. It had blue-grey feathers and very small useless wings.

Operation Tiger

There are thousands of species of animals that we have lost for ever, and today there are many more species that are close to extinction. In 1972 the magnificent Indian tiger was one of these.

As always, people were the cause of this: hunters who killed the tigers for their valuable skin or for 'sport', and farmers who destroyed the tiger's natural habitat. The number of tigers in India which had been 40,000 in 1900, went down to 2,000 in 1972.

In 1973 the World Wide Fund for Nature and the Indian government set up *Operation Tiger* to save this creature. They chose nine places where tigers could breed in safety and created special reserves there. The first was at Ranthambhore, an area which had only fourteen tigers left.

The government closed down twelve villages and moved the

CLAWING BACK
India's tiger population
1900 – 40,000 tigers
1972 – 2,000 tigers
1983 – 4,000 tigers
1989 – 5,000 tigers (estimate)

1,000 people that had lived there from the area. But they were not forgotten and the government provided new villages complete with temples, schools and fresh water supplies.
Now there are many other animals at Ranthambhore, like deer, monkeys and peacocks. And the reserve has more than forty tigers in the park. With over 5,000 tigers in all of India the future of the tiger looks more secure.

Language focus: RELATIVE CLAUSES

C
Look at the text again and match the subjects with the relative clauses.

Subject	Relative clause
1 species of animals	a) who killed the tigers
2 the number of tigers	b) that are close to extinction
	c) which had been 40,000 in 1900
3 an area	d) that we have lost forever
4 nine places	e) that had lived there
5 species	f) which had only fourteen tigers left
6 hunters	g) where tigers could breed in safety
7 the 1,000 people	

D
Complete the rules about relative clauses with *who*, *which*, *where* or *that*.

We use . . . or . . . for people and . . . or . . . for things or animals. We use . . . and . . . for places.

E
Complete the definitions with *who*, *that*, *which*, or *where*.

Example: 1 a person *who* hunts animals or birds = hunter

1 a person . . . . . hunts animals or birds
2 a person . . . . . owns or works on a farm
3 a sweet liquid . . . . . bees collect from flowers
4 a place . . . . . wild animals live and are protected

F
Find three definitions in the mini-dictionary which have relative pronouns. In groups, read out the definitions. See if the others can guess the words.

Nature project

G
Choose five animals from your country and write definitions.

Example: a very small bird which moves its wings very quickly and eats nectar

61

28 Revision

Listening

A

Listen to a recording from a nature watch project. Write notes about the different seasons.

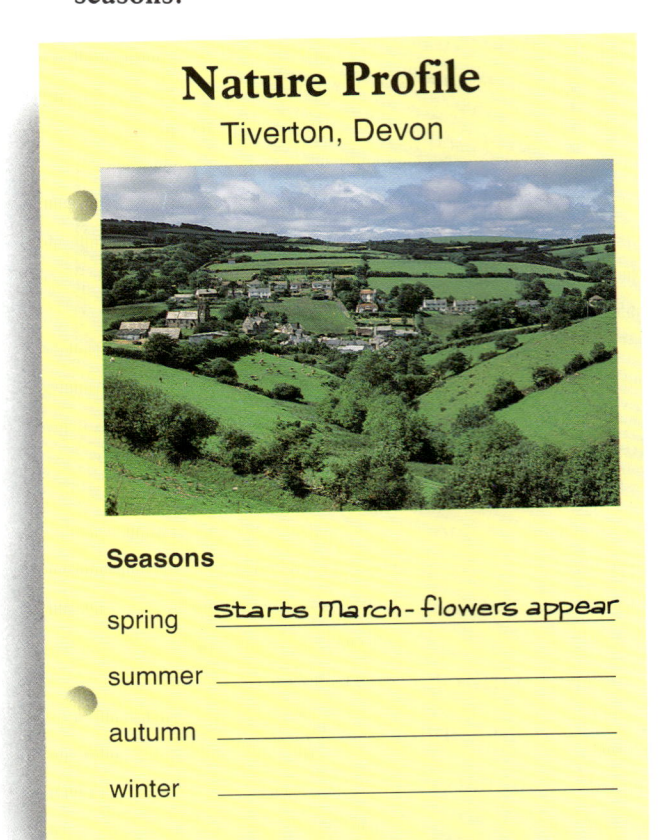

Nature Profile
Tiverton, Devon

Seasons

spring — Starts March - flowers appear

summer — _____

autumn — _____

winter — _____

Speaking

B

In pairs, what do you think will happen? Discuss the situations below.

Example: "I think the world's climate will change if we destroy the rainforest."

- If we destroy the rainforest...
- If the world's climate changes...
- If we destroy the ozone layer...
- If we continue polluting the seas and rivers...
- If there is a third world war...

C

In groups, Student A chooses an animal. The others ask questions with adjectives to find out what it is.

Example: B: Is it dangerous?
A: Yes, it is.
C: Is it more dangerous than a shark?
A: No, it isn't.
D: Is it faster than a tiger?
A: Yes, it is.
B: Is it the fastest animal in the world?
A: Yes, it is.
C: Is it a . . . ?

Language revision

D

Complete the description with these words:

who / which / that / where

They are pets [1] . . . . . are exotic, but easy to keep. You can feed the insects on leaves [2] . . . . . you can get in your garden. They are animals [3] . . . . . are clean and [4] . . . . . you don't have to take for a walk! Friends [5] . . . . . come to your house can watch your insects change colour. The insects come from countries [6] . . . . . they are very common, so you are not destroying a species.

E

Find three grammatical and three spelling mistakes and correct them.

A lot of people is afraid of spiders. They think they are the more sinister and dangerous creatures in the world. Some spiders are dangerous becos they are very poisnous. The redback spider in Australia who lives in houses can kill humans. But 99% of spiders are not dangerous and they are very usefull.

Learner training

F
Look at these phonetic symbols.

1 n*o*t /ɒ/   2 s*o*me /ʌ/   3 s*o* /əʊ/
    4 t*oo* /u:/   5 n*o*rmal /ɔ:/

Use the mini-dictionary to check the sounds in *italics* in the words below.

Example: c*u*t = /kʌt/ = 2

c*u*t   bl*oo*d   helic*o*pter   st*o*mach   sl*o*th
poll*u*tion   *o*zone   aer*o*sol   cl*aw*   cart*oo*n
br*o*ther   cl*o*se   p*o*rt   b*eau*tiful   b*oa*rd
h*u*mmingbird   n*u*clear   em*o*tion   h*o*ver

G
Look through words from this module in your vocabulary book. Mark words which have the sounds listed in exercise F. Check that you have marked the word stress.

Example: brochure = /brəʊʃə/

Nature project

H
Work in pairs or groups.

Stage 1 Decide if you want to produce a poster, magazine or radio programme (you will need a cassette recorder).
Stage 2 Collect all the project material you have from the module.
Stage 3 Select the best material. Check it and write final versions.
Stage 4 Add these things from your area: photos, drawings, leaves (if it is autumn).

I
Look at the Module Check on page 107.

Language check

SUPERLATIVES

The hummingbird is the **smallest** bird in the world.
The **most dangerous** shark is the Great White.
The **best** experts at disguise are stick and leaf insects.

FUTURE CONDITIONALS

If they **destroy** the rain forest, the climate **will** change.
If we **don't protect** the Taku sloth, it **will** disappear.
What **will** happen to the island **if** they **do** that?

RELATIVE CLAUSES

The government moved the people **who/that** had lived there.
They chose nine places **where** tigers could breed in safety.
There are many more species **which/that** are close to extinction.

MODULE 5 SPORT 29 The world of sport

A
Match the sports with the photos.

gymnastics / windsurfing / rugby / hang gliding

B LEARN TO LEARN
In pairs, copy the network below and classify these sports:

parachuting / hockey / tennis / basketball / golf / horse riding / canoeing / climbing / swimming / table tennis / football / skateboarding / skiing / sailing / athletics / judo / cycling / squash / skating / water skiing / volleyball / karate

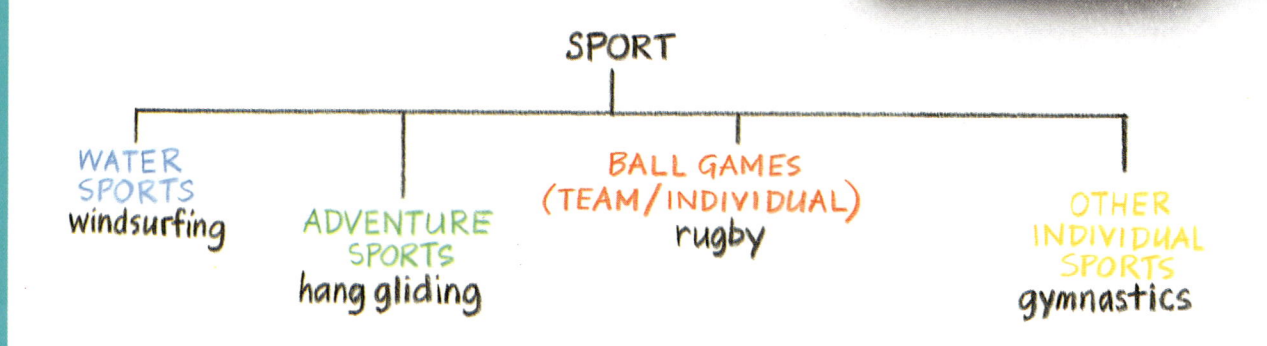

```
                        SPORT
       ┌──────────┬──────────┬──────────┬──────────┐
   WATER        ADVENTURE   BALL GAMES         OTHER
   SPORTS       SPORTS      (TEAM/INDIVIDUAL)  INDIVIDUAL
   windsurfing  hang gliding  rugby             SPORTS
                                                gymnastics
```

C

Look at these sentences:

1 You *go* swimming.
2 You *play* football.
3 You *do* athletics.

Which verb do we use for:
a) ball games?
b) most sports ending in *-ing*?
c) other sports?

Write five sentences about yourself.

Example: I often do gymnastics after school. I sometimes play tennis at the weekend. I go swimming in the summer.

D

In pairs, ask your partner these questions and write down his/her answers.

1 Which sport(s) has your partner watched?
2 Which sport(s) has he/she tried?
3 Which sport(s) does he/she do often?
4 Which sport(s) does he/she think is/are the most exciting to do?
5 Which sport(s) does he/she think is/are the most exciting to watch?
6 Which sport(s) has he/she not done but would like to try?
7 Which sport(s) would he/she never do because it is too dangerous?
8 Which sport(s) does he/she think is/are the most boring?

E

In groups, use your answers to calculate the most popular sport in the group.

Every time a sport is mentioned in answers 1 to 6, give it one point.
Every time it is mentioned in answers 7 and 8, take away three points.
Tell the rest of the class which is the most and least popular sport in your group.
Which is the most popular sport in the class?

F

In groups, one person thinks of a sport and the others have to guess which it is. You only have ten *yes/no* questions. Guess this sport:

B: Is it a team game? A: No, it isn't.
C: Do you use a ball? A: No, you don't.
D: Do you race? A: No, you don't.
B: Is it competitive? A: Yes, it is, sometimes.
C: Do you do exercises? A: Yes, you do.
D: Is it . . . ? A: Yes, it is.

G

Amazing but false. Only one of these facts is true. Which one is it?

A The Vikings used to play a kind of football, using a ball made of cloth.

B The highest ever football score was achieved by Sporting de Santa Cruz against Atlético Tarija on 3rd September 1947. They won 28–0.

C There is a village in England where every year there is a sheep race. The sheep have to go over small jumps.

D The first basketball in space was played on 21st February 1989 by eight Russian cosmonauts on the Soyuz space station.

E The American swimmer Mark Spitz won ten gold medals in the 1972 Olympic Games.

30 I hate sport!

How sporty are you?

1 How often do you do sport every week?
a) two or three times
b) never
c) every day

2 On a cold wet Sunday afternoon what would you prefer to do?
a) watch sport on TV
b) go to the cinema
c) go out and play games

3 How much can you remember about the last Olympics?
a) nothing
b) the names of two gold medal winners
c) the names of ten or more gold medal winners

4 During the last Olympics, which of these things did you do?
a) you did your homework very quickly to watch it
b) you didn't do any homework and watched everything
c) you didn't watch any of it

5 Do you look forward to your P.E. lessons at school?
a) No, I hate them!
b) Not very much.
c) Yes, I love them!

6 Which of these things have you got in your bedroom?
a) lots of sports posters and books
b) only one or two sports posters
c) no sports books or posters

7 Have you ever dreamed about your favourite sport?
a) never
b) sometimes
c) often

Did you know?

Johnny Weissmuller won three swimming gold medals at the 1924 Paris Olympics. He later became even more famous, as the cinema's first Tarzan.

8 **Are you going to play sport this weekend?**
   a) yes
   b) possibly
   c) no

Points
1 a) 1	b) 0	c) 2
2 a) 1	b) 0	c) 2
3 a) 0	b) 1	c) 3
4 a) 1	b) 2	c) 0
5 a) 0	b) 1	c) 2
6 a) 2	b) 1	c) 0
7 a) 0	b) 1	c) 2
8 a) 2	b) 1	c) 0

Results
Less than 5 points:
   You hate sport!!
5–10 points:
   You quite like sport.
More than 10 points:
   You are a sports fanatic!

A
Read the questionnaire. Think about your answers.

B
In pairs, interview your partner and find out his/her score.

C
Listen to Sheila and Alan. Write down their answers to the questionnaire and calculate their points.

Language focus: AGREEING AND DISAGREEING

D
Listen again. How do they agree and disagree with each other? Complete the sentences in the box.

	Agreement
1 I do it two or three times.	So do I.
2 I wouldn't go to the cinema.	Neither . . . . .
3 I can remember about two or three.	So . . . . .
4 I don't look forward to P.E.	Neither . . . . .
5 I've got a couple of posters.	So . . . . .
6 I'm definitely not going to.	Neither . . . . .
	Disagreement
7 I would watch sport on TV.	I wouldn't.
8 I didn't watch anything.	I . . . . .
9 I've never dreamed about playing.	I . . . . .

E
Use the words below to complete the rule for agreeing and disagreeing.

neither / nor / so

We use . . . . . to agree with affirmative statements, and . . . . . or . . . . . to agree with negative statements.

Pronunciation

F
Which 'I' is stressed, the first one or the second one?

Statement   *Reply*
1 I love watching basketball.   So do I.

Listen to the example again. Write down the key words.

Example: 1 love / basketball / I

Then listen again and repeat the replies.

G
In groups, say sentences about yourself. Find out how many people are like you.

Example: A: I love playing tennis.   B: So do I.   C: I don't.

67

31 Champions

She won four gold medals at the age of fourteen!

The greatest footballer this century.

She played seventy-four consecutive tennis matches without losing.

One of the most brilliant athletes ever.

A
Match the names with the photos.
Martina Navratilova / Pele / Carl Lewis / Nadia Comaneci

B
In groups, who do you think is the best now? Choose one player or team for each sport. Then say what you think and find out who agrees with you.

Example: A: I think that . . . . . is the best player in the world now!
B: So do I.
C: I don't.
D: I don't.

Tell the rest of the class who the group thinks are the best players and teams now.

68

C
Read about Pele. Copy and complete the timeline.

```
1....              scored brilliant goal       Mexico World Cup        5....
1940 _____ 1958 _____ 1961 __ 1962 _____ 1966 _____ 1970 _____ 1974 __ 1975
       2....           Chile World Cup  3....                  4....
```

Edson Arantes do Nascimento was born in 1940 in the small Brazilian town of Tres Curaçoes. Young Edson was like many Brazilian boys and he could kick a football almost before he could walk. He grew up spending hours playing football in the street with his friends.

It was when he was playing for the local youth teams that people noticed that there was something very special about young Edson. At 16 the first division club Santos took him on as a professional and young Edson's incredible career had begun.

As a professional he became known as Pele and the name Pele was soon famous throughout the world. When he was seventeen he played for the Brazilian national team and with several brilliant goals he helped his team to win the World Cup in Sweden, in 1958. In 1961 he scored probably the most spectacular goal ever, when he beat the entire opposition team before scoring.

In the 1962 World Cup in Chile he was injured after two games, but Brazil won again. In 1966 he had to leave the World Cup in England early because he was injured. But he went on to play for a superb Brazil side in Mexico in 1970, to win the World Cup for a third time. In 1974 he retired, but came back the next year to play for the New York Cosmos for a record $7,000,000.

During his career Pele scored 1,217 goals in 1,254 games, an incredible achievement. He became a hero not only in Brazil, but all over the world. In 1980 he was voted the Athlete of the Century. It is difficult to be better than that.

D
Now answer these questions.

1 When did he learn to play football?
2 Why was his goal in 1961 spectacular?
3 Why was the 1966 World Cup bad for Pele?
4 What was his last club?

E
Try to guess the correct definitions of these words from the context in the article.

1 grow up (line 5)
  a) to happen
  b) to develop from a child to a man or woman

2 take on (line 10)
  a) to start a fight with someone
  b) to employ someone

3 go on (line 25)
  a) to continue doing something
  b) to happen

4 come back (line 28)
  a) to remember something that happened before
  b) to return

F
Mini-dictionary game. Look through the mini-dictionary and find two words that you don't know. Write down the definitions. Then invent two other definitions for each word and write them down. In groups read out the correct and the false definitions. The others must guess which is the correct one.

Example: crop = *verb* look hard and unpleasantly at someone
        noun food that is grown
        noun something that children play with

69

32 Clubs

Richards Castle Sports Club

Application Form

Date: _1st March_

Surname: _Abayawickrama_   Forename(s): _Naima_

Address: _Green Farm, Orleton_

Date of birth: _____   Sex: male / female (circle)

Sports: _____

Previous experience: _____

Competitions/teams: _____

Do you want coaching sessions? (specify) _____

A
In pairs, list the places where you can play sport in your town or city.

Example: school / municipal swimming pool

B
Copy the form. Then listen and complete it.

Did you know?
In her career, Billie Jean King won a record twenty Wimbledon titles. She also set up the Women's Sports Foundation to increase opportunities for women and girls in sport.

Language focus: QUESTION TAGS

C
Listen again and match each sentence with the correct question tag.

Affirmative or negative sentences	Question tags
1 Your full name is Naima Abawickrama	a) are you?
2 You don't live in Richards Castle,	b) didn't you?
3 You aren't sixteen yet,	c) isn't it?
4 You want to play squash,	d) do you?
5 You were in your school swimming team last year,	e) have you?
6 You won the school 100m freestyle race,	f) don't you?
7 You've never played squash before,	g) weren't you?

D
Copy and complete the rule.

In a negative sentence the question tag is . . . . .
In an affirmative sentence the question tag is . . . . .

Pronunciation

E
We use question tags to check information we already know.

Falling intonation:
Your full name is Naima Abawickrama, isn't it?

Or we use question tags to check information we are not sure about.

Rising intonation:
He plays in the squash team, doesn't he?

Listen to the question tags and decide which are checking information we already know and which are checking information we are not sure about. Listen and repeat them.

F
In pairs, imagine you are applying to join a sports club. Copy the application form in exercise B again and complete it for yourself. Give the form to your partner. He/she checks it, like this:

A: Your name is . . . . . , isn't it?
B: Yes, it is.

G
Question tag game. In pairs, Student A makes a statement. Student B adds the question tag.

A: You don't like football . . . ,
B: . . . do you?
B: Last week she joined the club . . . ,
C: . . . didn't she?

H
Play the question tag game in groups of six. Two pairs play and one pair act as referees.

PAIR A: We're playing tennis tomorrow . . . ,
PAIR B: . . . aren't we?
PAIR B: I've never played basketball . . . ,
PAIR A: . . . have I?

For every correct question tag you get two points. If you answer incorrectly or take more than ten seconds, the other team gets two points. After five minutes stop and see who the winners are.

33 Warming up

A
Match these words with the parts of the body in the picture.

leg / arm / head / foot / hand / mouth / face

Write down the new words in your vocabulary book.

B
Listen to this P.E. expert, Jean Alford, giving advice.

1. What sports does she mention?
2. What parts of the body does she mention?

C
Listen again. True or false?

1. You should warm up, because if you don't you can get serious injuries.
2. You should jog and run to increase your circulation.
3. For football you should do exercises to relax your arms.
4. You should not put anything on after doing exercise, because you can get very hot.
5. You should not do exercise immediately after a big meal.

D
Use the table below to write sentences giving advice with *because* and *to*. Look at the examples in exercise C.

Advice	Why?
Football: do exercises	stretch legs
Tennis: do exercises	relax arms
Do not wear bad shoes	they can injure your feet
Eat carbohydrates	give you energy

Example: For football you should do exercises to stretch your legs.

E
In pairs, match the diagrams with the instructions. Then do the exercises!

Warm up for English!

You can do these exercises while you are sitting down, before your English class (not in it!). They help you feel better and keep your muscles flexible.

1 First put your fingers together and then put your arms out in front of you for twenty seconds. This is good to relax your arms.

2 Hold on to your left leg below the knee. After that pull it upwards and hold it for thirty seconds. Do both legs. This is good for your legs.

3 People may think you are strange when you do this! Raise your eyebrows and then open your mouth wide and stick your tongue out. Hold this position for five to ten seconds. This is good for relaxing your face and will make you smile!

F
In pairs, invent your own warming up exercise.

Stage 1 Draw simple diagrams of the exercises, like these:

Stage 2 Make notes of the different stages in the exercise.

Example: 1 stand up
2 put arms out in front
3 hold this position for thirty seconds

Stage 3 Use your notes to write instructions.
(Include words like *first / then / after that*)

G
In groups, read out your instructions to the other pair. Decide what sport the exercise would be good for.

Did you know?

Surfing is an ancient Polynesian sport. The first European to see it was Captain Cook when he visited Tahiti in 1771.

34 Armchair sport

TV GUIDE

BBC 1

2.00 **The Clothes Show:** Teenagers talk about buying clothes

2.30 **Tennis:** The Australian Open. Sabatini v Sanchez Graf v Novotna

5.15 **Cartoons:** Tom and Jerry

6.00 **News**

BBC 2

2.30 **Basketball:** NBA games. Detroit Pistons v Boston Celtics

3.15 **Way West** (film 1967)**:** A cowboy film with Kirk Douglas, Robert Mitchum and Richard Widmark

5.00 **Rugby Special:** Scotland v Wales/Ireland v France

6.00 **Ski Sunday:** The World Championships from Saalbach, Austria

Channel 4

2.00 **The Winslow Boy** (film 1948)

4.10 **Czech cartoons**

4.30 **News Summary**

4.40 **Scottish Eye:** 'Fowl Play': poisoning of rare birds in Scotland

5.30 **The Waltons:** The Silver Wings

ITV

2.00 **Charlie's Angels** (*repeat*)**:** Guest stars Kate Jackson and Cheryl Ladd

2.55 **The Match:** Manchester Utd v Liverpool. Football from Old Trafford

5.05 **International Athletics:** The Assurance National Indoor Championships from Cosworth

6.35 **Golf:** New Zealand Open from Auckland

A

In pairs, find out what sports programmes your partner watches on television. What is his/her favourite sports programme?

B

In pairs, read the television guide and plan an afternoon's viewing. How many hours of sport are you going to watch?

C

Listen to two commentaries. Which of the sporting events in the TV guide are they from?

Language focus: ADVERBS

D

Listen to the commentaries again. Look at the list below and write down which adverbs you hear.

never / slowly / happily / nervously / occasionally / hard / quickly / fast / desperately / often / nearly / angrily / bravely / well / clearly / noisily / calmly / beautifully / completely / suddenly / usually

Which of the adverbs are adverbs of frequency?

Example: never, . . .

E

What letters do you add to adjectives to form regular adverbs?
Look at the adverbs above and use them to complete these tables.

Regular adverbs		Irregular adverbs
+ -ly	+ -ily	hard
badly	happily	

F

Complete the text with the adverbs below. Read the whole text before you start!

happily / gradually / never / slowly / nervously / fast / sadly / always

Before races Manuela [1] . . . . . felt nervous. But she had [2] . . . . . felt like this before. She walked out [3] . . . . . into the stadium. She waited [4] . . . . . for the race to start.

The race started and in the first few metres she saw her American rival running [5] . . . . . in front of her. She began to catch up with her [6] . . . . . With ten metres to go they were level and Manuela won by a few centimetres. She smiled [7] . . . . . at the crowd as the American walked away [8] . . . . . .

G

Adverb game. One person chooses one of the adverbs below.

slowly / nervously / quietly / violently / calmly / fast / happily / sadly

Then he/she does something in the the way the adverb describes. Choose actions, like these:

stand up / open your book / say something, etc.

The others must guess the adverb.

Did you know?

The highest speed recorded on a skateboard was 115.53 kilometres an hour by Richard K Brown in California.

35 Revision

Listening

A

Can you answer these questions?

1 Where were the Olympic Games in 1896?
2 What country won the football World Cup in 1970?
3 What is the name of the oldest and most important tennis championships in the world?
4 How many rings are there in the Olympic symbol?
5 What was the name of the Romanian gymnast who won four gold medals at the age of fourteen?

Listen to the sports quiz and check your answers.

Speaking

B

Check what you know about your partner. Ask five questions.

Example: You've got two brothers, haven't you?

C

Copy-cat game. In groups of four, one person says something about their life.

Example: A: I watched TV last night.

If the others do or did the same they agree and get one point. If you make a mistake you get no points.

Example: B: So did I.

After five minutes, stop and see who has the most points. You must tell the truth!

Language revision

D

Match these tenses with the sentences. Then write a question beginning with the word in brackets.

Present simple / Past simple /
Present continuous / Past continuous /
Present perfect / Past perfect

Example: 1 They like athletics. Present simple
What do they like?

1 They like athletics. (What . . . ?)
2 He scored two goals. (How many . . . ?)
3 They have gone to the match. (Where . . . ?)
4 She had learned karate. (What . . . ?)
5 She is playing tennis. (What . . . ?)
6 They were playing badly. (How . . . ?)

E

Use the adverbs below to rewrite the description. The adverbs are in the right order. Be sure to put them in the right place.

Example: Bob plays hockey very badly.

1 very badly	6 slowly
2 often	7 usually
3 hard	8 completely
4 fast	9 unhappily
5 accurately	10 angrily

Bob plays hockey.¹ On Sundays he goes² with his sister Leslie to practise in the park. She is in her school team and she can hit³ the ball. She can run⁴ and pass⁵ the ball. Bob is the opposite. He runs⁶ and when he tries to hit the ball he⁷ misses⁸. After the practice session Bob walks⁹ home. He hits¹⁰ his stick on the ground and says: 'Next time I'll do it!'

76

Learner training

F [LEARN TO LEARN]

In which situation do you speak English?

1 talking to a tourist in your town or city
2 answering the telephone
3 having a conversation with an English-speaking person of your age
4 doing a speaking activity in class with your partner
5 buying something in a shop when you are on holiday abroad
6 speaking English in front of the class
7 talking with someone who speaks English as their second language
8 speaking to your teacher in the lesson

Mark the situations out of ten for difficulty.

Example: $2 = \frac{9}{10}$

In the future will you use your English in any other situations?

G [LEARN TO LEARN]

Look at the situations below. Match them with the correct sentence.

buying things / expressing opinions / agreeing / making arrangements / checking information / telling stories / inviting

a) 'What are you doing on Saturday night?'
b) 'You're thirteen, aren't you?'
c) 'When we were having lunch, we saw a . . .'
d) 'Would you like to come to the cinema?'
e) 'How much is it?'
f) 'So do I.'
g) 'I think it's a bad idea because . . .'

How good are you at each situation? Give yourself a mark out of 5 for each one.

5 – No problems! I never make mistakes.
4 – I only occasionally make mistakes.
3 – I sometimes have problems with it but I can communicate what I want to.
2 – I often make mistakes and I hesitate a lot.
1 – I can't do this!

Writing

H

Imagine that you have to describe a sport to a Martian.

I

Look at the module check on page 107.

Language check

AGREEING

A: I really love playing.
B: **So do I.**
A: I can't play very well.
B: **Nor/Neither can I.**
A: I didn't enjoy the match.
B: **Nor/Neither did I.** It was boring.

DISAGREEING

A: I love swimming.
B: **I don't.** I hate it.
A: I don't like tennis.
B: **I do.** I play every week.
A: I enjoyed the match.
B: **I didn't.** It was terrible.

QUESTION TAGS

Your name is Naima, **isn't it?**
You aren't sixteen, **are you?**
He plays in the squash team, **doesn't he?**

ADVERBS

Regular
She walked **slowly** out into the stadium.
They smiled **happily** at the crowd.

Irregular
We tried very **hard**.
He was running **well**.

MODULE 6
SPACE
36 Our solar system

A
Match the planets with the letters on the diagram.

Pluto / Mars / Jupiter / Earth / Mercury / Saturn / Venus

Now read the text and check your answers.

B
Match each paragraph with the best title.

- The Outer Planets
- The Inner Planets
- Our Sun

C
Answer these questions.

1. What is our galaxy called?
2. How hot is the sun?
3. How long is a year on Mercury?
4. Why is it so hot on Venus?
5. Why did people use to think there was life on Mars?
6. What special features can we see on Jupiter and Saturn?
7. How long is a year on Pluto?

[1] Have you ever tried to count the stars in the night sky? Nobody knows how many there are. A group of stars is called a galaxy, and there are millions of galaxies in the universe. Our sun is one of the smallest stars on the edge of our galaxy, the Milky Way. Imagine the sun is one grain of sand. Now add a bucket of sand to it – that represents the stars in the Milky Way. Now try to imagine how many buckets of sand there are in the Sahara desert, and you have an idea of how many stars there are in the universe!

[2] Let's imagine a tour of our solar system. We begin our journey from the sun, but of course we could never live there – the temperature on the surface is 6000° C! The first planet we see is Mercury. It is strange because the

D

Find words in the text which mean the following:

1 One of the large objects like the Earth that go round the sun.
2 A mixture of gases that surrounds a planet.
3 Any of the large groups of stars which make up the universe.
4 Goes round.

E

How old are you on Earth and on Mercury?

Example: If you are ten:
Ten Earth years
= 10 × 365 = 3650 days
One Mercury year = 88 days
So, 3650 ÷ 88 = 41: You're about 41 Mercury years old!

How old is your mother/sister/teacher on Mercury? Tell the class.

Example: My mother's about 145!

F

Invent a new planet. Copy the table below and fill in the information for your planet.

Name	Jupiter
Size	very big
Moons/Rings	16 moons
Distance from Sun	780 million km
Length of Year	11.9 Earth years

In pairs, ask questions to find out about your partner's planet.

Example: What's it called?
How big is it?
How many . . . ?
How far . . . ?
How long . . . ?

same side always faces the sun, so one half of the planet is very hot and the other extremely cold. It orbits the sun once every 88 days. The next planet we see is cloudy Venus. The thick gases in its atmosphere have created a 'greenhouse effect', with temperatures of up to 500° C during the day! (The highest temperature recorded on Earth is 57° C in Death Valley.) Our Earth is the next planet we pass on our journey. We think it is the only planet with life. After Earth is Mars. People used to think there was life on Mars because they thought they could see 'canals' on its surface. We now know this is not true.

3 The next four planets are giants. Jupiter, the next stop on our tour, has a mysterious 'red spot' on its surface. This spot, which moves, is many times bigger than our Earth! Next is Saturn, famous for its colourful rings of rock and ice which go round it. A person standing on Saturn and looking up at the rings would see a beautiful rainbow in the sky. We know very little about the next two giant planets, Uranus and Neptune, and even less about tiny Pluto, the furthest planet from the sun. Pluto takes 248 Earth years to go round the sun!

37 Science fact or fiction?

A
Match the pictures with the captions.

- Meet aliens
- Use suspended animation
- Travel at the speed of light
- Build a space colony
- Land on another planet

B
In groups, discuss which things are possible now. Which do you think we will do in the future? Tell the class.

Example: We think we will meet aliens.
We think we can land on another planet now.

C
Listen to Dr Edith Lanfear, a science expert, talking about ideas in science-fiction. In what order does she mention the ideas in exercise A?

Dr Edith Lanfear

80

Language focus:
TALKING ABOUT THE FUTURE

D
Listen again. Look at this extract and complete Dr Lanfear's answers with the words below.

will / might / may / won't

INTERVIEWER:	Do you think we will ever meet aliens?
DR LANFEAR:	Well, there's a possibility. We [1]..... meet some one day.
INTERVIEWER:	Do you think we will ever land on another planet?
DR LANFEAR:	Yes, we certainly [2].....
INTERVIEWER:	Do you think we will ever build space colonies?
DR LANFEAR:	Oh yes. I'm sure we [3]..... one day. Scientists from Nasa have already designed one.
INTERVIEWER:	Do you think we will ever travel at the speed of light?
DR LANFEAR:	No, we [4]..... It's quite impossible.
INTERVIEWER:	Do you think we will ever use suspended animation?
DR LANFEAR:	Well, we have made some progress with this idea. We [5]..... one day.

E
Look at the box and answer the questions.

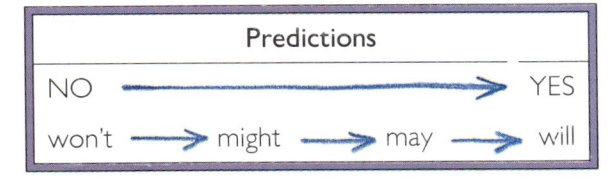

```
              Predictions
  NO  ─────────────────────────▶  YES
  won't ──▶ might ──▶ may ──▶ will
```

1. Which words express:
   a) positive certainty?
   b) negative certainty?   c) possibility?
2. Which word expresses a less certain possibility, *may* or *might*?

F
Use the ideas below and write sentences about what you think will happen in your lifetime.

Example: There will/might/may/won't be mines on the Moon.

- mines on the Moon
- colonies in space
- Olympic sports in space
- a war with aliens

Add two more sentences of your own.

G
In groups, take turns to ask questions about the future.

Example: A: Do you think there will be schools in space?
B: Yes, I think there will.
C: No, there won't.
D: Well, there may be one day.

Pronunciation

H
Listen to these words from the lesson. Mark the stress. Listen again. Mark the sound /ə/.

Example: 1 ólder

1 older	4 another	7 popular
2 animation	5 technology	8 colony
3 ever	6 science	

In pairs, find five more words from this module which contain the sound /ə/. Exchange your list with another pair and mark the main stress and the sound /ə/.

Did you know?

In the future, satellites may collect solar power and send the power to Earth.

38 Your stars

A
Very quickly, look at the pictures and texts in this lesson. What is this lesson about, *astrology* or *astronomy*? Check any words you don't know in the mini-dictionary.

B
Read about the four elements (*Earth*, *Air*, *Fire* and *Water*) and decide which one describes you.

C
Read the texts again. Find five adjectives that describe personality and write them in your vocabulary book.

Example: creative

D
Find words or expressions in the texts which link ideas.

Example: Creative *and* dynamic . . .
They are *also* . . .

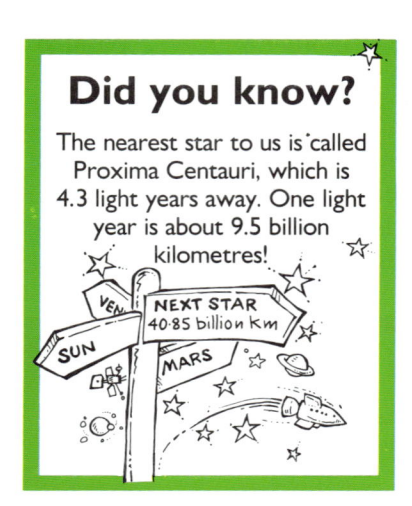

Did you know?
The nearest star to us is called Proxima Centauri, which is 4.3 light years away. One light year is about 9.5 billion kilometres!

FIRE
Fire is the first of the four signs. People born under fire signs are creative and dynamic. They are also enthusiastic, energetic and show initiative.

WATER
People born under these signs are emotional and passionate. Their feelings dominate them and they often do things without thinking.

AIR
Air is the element of reason. Besides being rational and logical, people born under these signs are often good at organising, analysing or expressing ideas.

EARTH
People born under this sign are the most practical. As well as being practical, people of these signs like material things and security.

E
What elements do these people belong to?

Example: 1 Paul = Earth

1 Paul is practical. He is good at organising.
2 Robert is dynamic. He has a lot of initiative and energy.
3 Christine is emotional. She often acts without thinking.
4 Sarah is very practical. She likes material things.
5 Charlotte is very logical. She is good at expressing ideas.

F
Rewrite the sentences in exercise E using the expressions below. Use a different expression for each sentence.

as well as / besides / and / also

Example: 1 *As well as* being practical, Paul is good at organising.

G

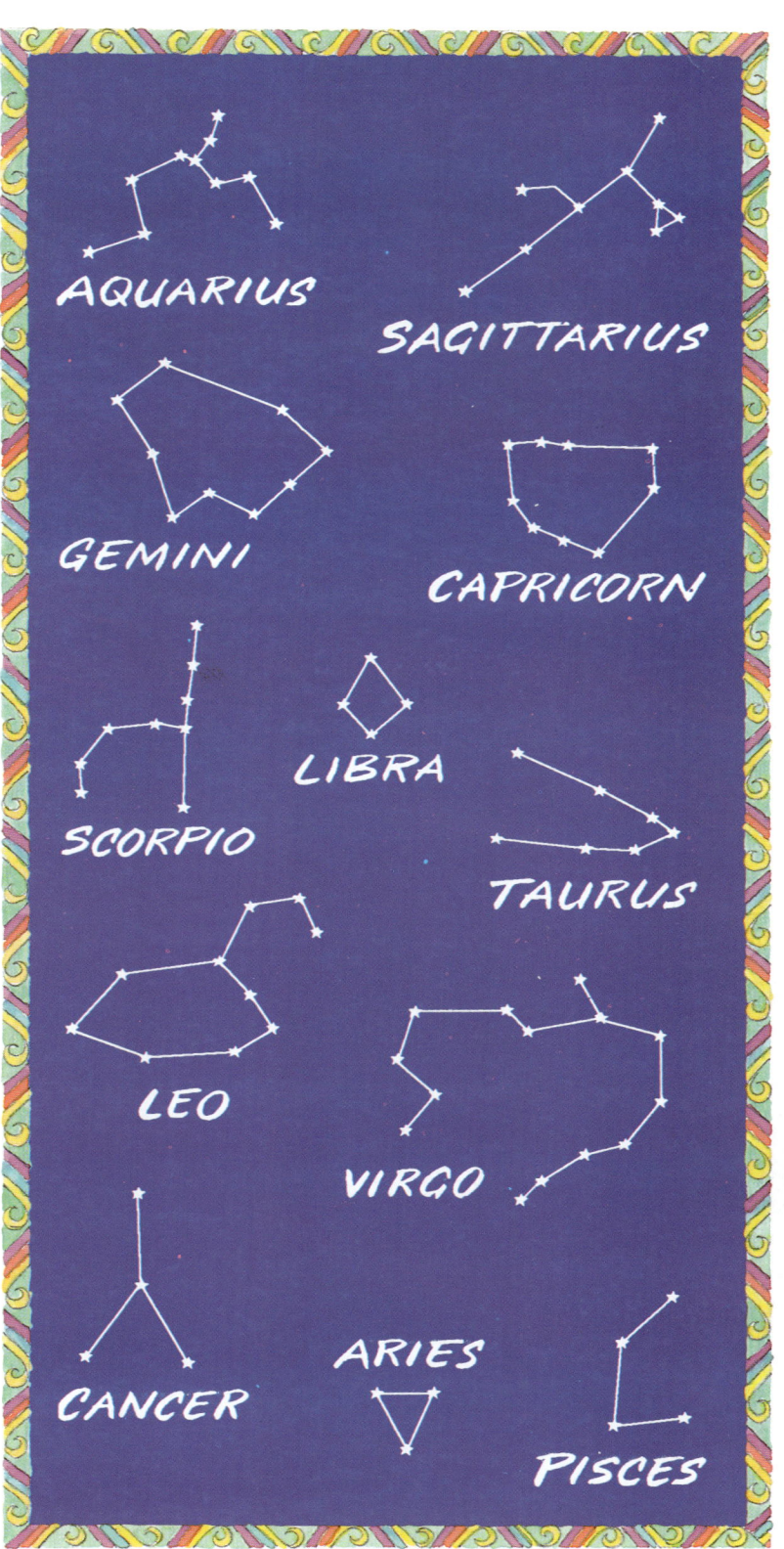

Perhaps stars influence our lives. Look at the stars. Which is your sign of the zodiac?

H

In pairs, write horoscopes for two signs of the zodiac, like this:

> *Taurus 21 April – 20 May*
> This week will not be very good for you. Besides having problems with one of your family, you will have an argument with one of your friends. As well as this, a teacher will get angry with you at school. Try to stay calm! The week will not be a good time for travelling, so do not go on any long journeys. On Thursday you must be careful with your money or you might lose some. However, it isn't all bad. On Saturday you will meet a very interesting person who might change your life!

I

Read your horoscopes to the class. When you hear your sign, agree or disagree.

Example: Yes, that may happen.
I'm sure I won't do that!

39 A space colony

A

Read the description of a space colony.
Make notes under these headings:

- transport
- sports
- food
- industry

Example: transport: monorail/rockets

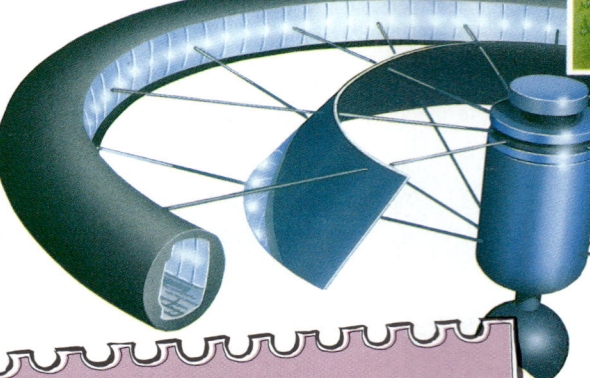

My space colony

Nebula Brown   Class 6C   20th Feb 2050

The colony where I live is called Lunar Taurus 12. It looks like a giant wheel turning in space. The spaceport, where rockets arrive and leave, is at the centre of the wheel. This is connected by monorails to the wheel itself where we live. The monorails are very quick and it doesn't take very long to get anywhere in the colony.

In the spaceport there are shops, a hotel and also a zero-gravity sports centre. You can practise 'flying' and you can play three-dimensional volleyball, which is my favourite game. Because there is no gravity, you can hit the ball under the net and bounce it off the ceiling!

There are 10,000 people on Lunar Taurus 12 and we all live on the inside of the wheel, where conditions are very similar to those on Earth. The wheel spins round and this creates artificial gravity. Giant mirrors direct sunlight onto the wheel and we have forests, fields and rivers just like on Earth. There's even an artificial beach with a wave-machine, so you can go surfing.

All our food is grown on the colony. We have special farms where all kinds of vegetables are grown (all the people on the colony are vegetarian). There are also many different factories on the colony. Rockets bring minerals from the Moon to them and everything from computers to toothpaste is manufactured here. There is a big factory near the colony where spaceships are manufactured and repaired. My father works there.

Nothing on the colony is wasted of course and everything is recycled. It is incredible to think that fifty years ago on Earth, people destroyed and threw away so many things!

Language focus:
PRESENT SIMPLE PASSIVE

B
Study the sentences in the box.

> 1 They recycle everything. (*Active*)
> 2 Everything is recycled. (*Passive*)
> 3 Rockets bring minerals from the Moon. (*Active*)
> 4 Minerals are brought from the Moon by rockets. (*Passive*)

What is the subject in each sentence?

Example: 1 = they

What is the verb?

Example: 1 = recycle

Now answer these questions.

1 The verb in the passive has two parts. What are they?
2 In sentence 2, do we know who recycles everything? Is it important?
3 In sentence 4, do we know what brings minerals from the Moon? Which is more important, the minerals or the rocket?
4 Which sentences from the box are used in the text?

C
Find more examples of passive sentences in the text.

D
Change these sentences from active to passive.

1 Mirrors direct sunlight onto the wheel.
2 They play three-dimensional space volleyball in the Zero-G sports centre.
3 This creates artificial gravity.
4 They grow all kinds of crops.

E
In groups, play this game. You need dice and counters. You have to go round the space colony once and then return to the spaceport. When you land on a square, you have to say a sentence using the passive. If you make a mistake, you miss a turn. When you land on a blank square, do nothing.

Example: A: (*lands on zoo square*) Earth animals are kept here.
B: (*lands on school square*) English are taught here. (*Wrong = miss a turn*)

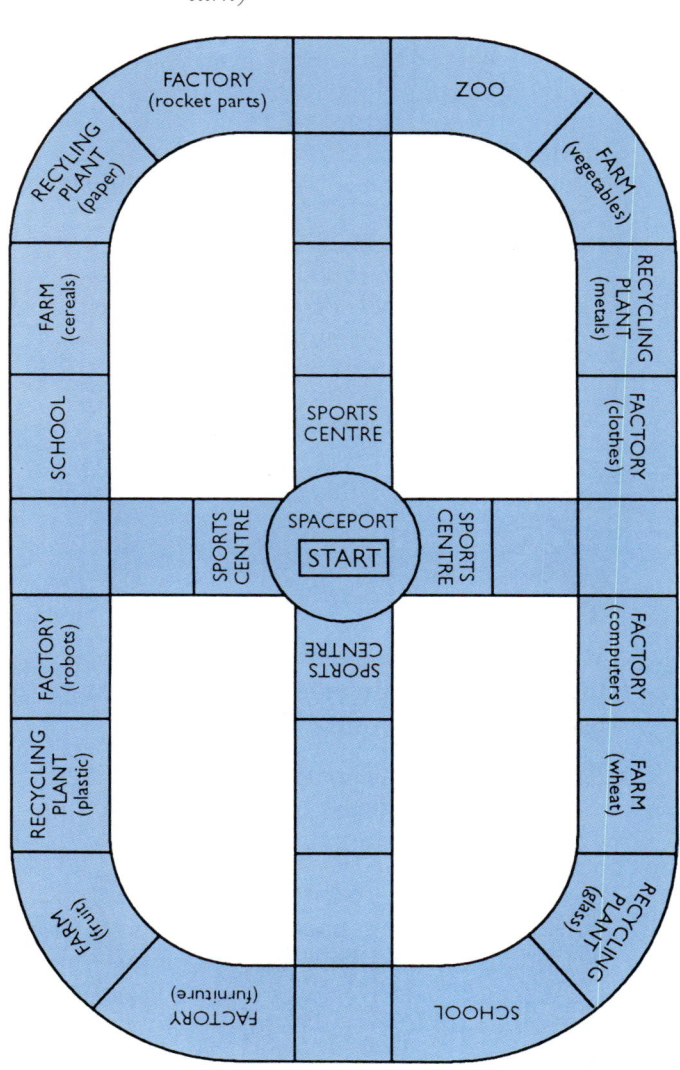

85

40 Marathon men

MARATHON MEN
EXCLUSIVE INTERVIEW

Cosmonauts Titov and Maranov returned to Earth on 21st December 1988 after a flight of 365 days, 22 hours, 39 minutes and 47 seconds.

INTERVIEWER: Why did you decide to become cosmonauts?
VLADIMIR: I was in the Soviet Air Force and it just happened.
MUSA: While I was *working* in an office in the Control Centre, I became a cosmonaut.
INTERVIEWER: Vladimir, on your *second* flight, with Gennady Strekalov, there was a fire and you narrowly escaped with your lives. Could you describe that?
VLADIMIR: Yes, with less than *two* minutes before launch the rocket caught fire. Ground control immediately decided to get us out. Maybe they will put me in the Book of Records for the shortest space flight as well!
INTERVIEWER: What do you remember about the launch of your marathon flight?
MUSA: It was a very *cold* day in Kazakhstan, a bit *misty*, but everything happened just like in training.
INTERVIEWER: You had a small doll with you for good luck, didn't you?
VLADIMIR: Something like that.
INTERVIEWER: Musa, Radio Moscow reported that you didn't *sleep* well. Was that because of zero-gravity?
MUSA: No, I never sleep very well the first night away from home.
INTERVIEWER: Could you describe a typical day in space?
MUSA: We used to wake up about 8 a.m. Then we washed, cleaned our teeth, shaved, had breakfast. After breakfast we used to work for three hours and then exercise for about an hour, then back to work, followed by lunch. After that, more work and exercise and finally supper.
INTERVIEWER: Could you describe re-entry and landing, and how it felt to be back?
MUSA: We had a delay of two orbits. You always feel worried because during re-entry there are a lot of vibrations – and a lot of noise! But it was a soft landing. It was difficult for us to climb out of the cabin because zero-gravity had put a lot of stress on our hearts.
INTERVIEWER: How soon after the landing did you recover?
MUSA: The moment we hit the ground we looked at each other and agreed that we felt pretty good!

A

Would you like to go into space? Which of the things below do you think might be a problem or dangerous? Tell the class.

Example: I think sleeping might be a problem because there is no day and night in space.

- sleeping
- taking off
- landing
- re-entering the atmosphere
- eating and drinking
- living in zero-gravity

B

Read the article and check your answers.

C

Read the article again and answer the questions below. Who did these things? Was it Vladimir (V), Musa (M) or Vladimir and Musa (V + M)?

1 Who went on possibly the shortest space flight?
2 Who nearly died in an accident?
3 Who took his little doll with him for luck?
4 Who didn't sleep very well?
5 Who woke up at 8a.m.?
6 Who had difficulty in getting out of the cabin?

D

Read and listen to three students acting out the first part of the interview. What mistakes do they make? The words in *italics* are different.

Example: studying not *working*

E

Write some diary notes for a three-day mission into space. Write about the launch, a typical day in space and the landing.

Stage 1 Make some notes for each day.
Stage 2 Check verb tenses and spellings.

Use the model below to help you.

MONDAY:
got up early – felt nervous – launch at 3pm – everything was OK – went outside rocket – saw the Earth – looked incredible – very colourful – zero-gravity is strange – I'm writing this on the ceiling!

F

Work in pairs. Student A, you are a journalist, student B, you are a cosmonaut who has just returned from space. Use your notes from exercise E and act out an interview, like this:

A: What do you remember about the launch?
B: Well, I felt very nervous and . . .

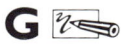

G

Choose one day from your diary and write the notes as full sentences.

Pronunciation

H

Look at the words below. Say them. Then listen to the cassette and repeat the words.

1 sky   skateboard   school   score
2 space   spaghetti   sport   speed
3 stretch strange   stress   strict
4 exercise expert   extinct   explain

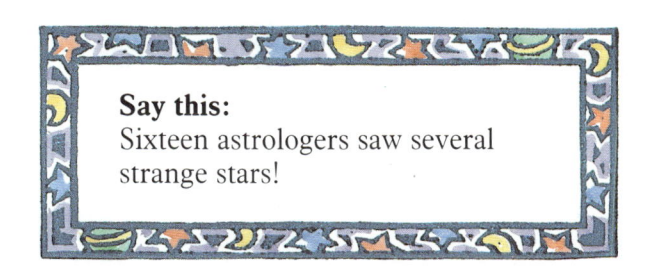

Say this:
Sixteen astrologers saw several strange stars!

41 Time travel

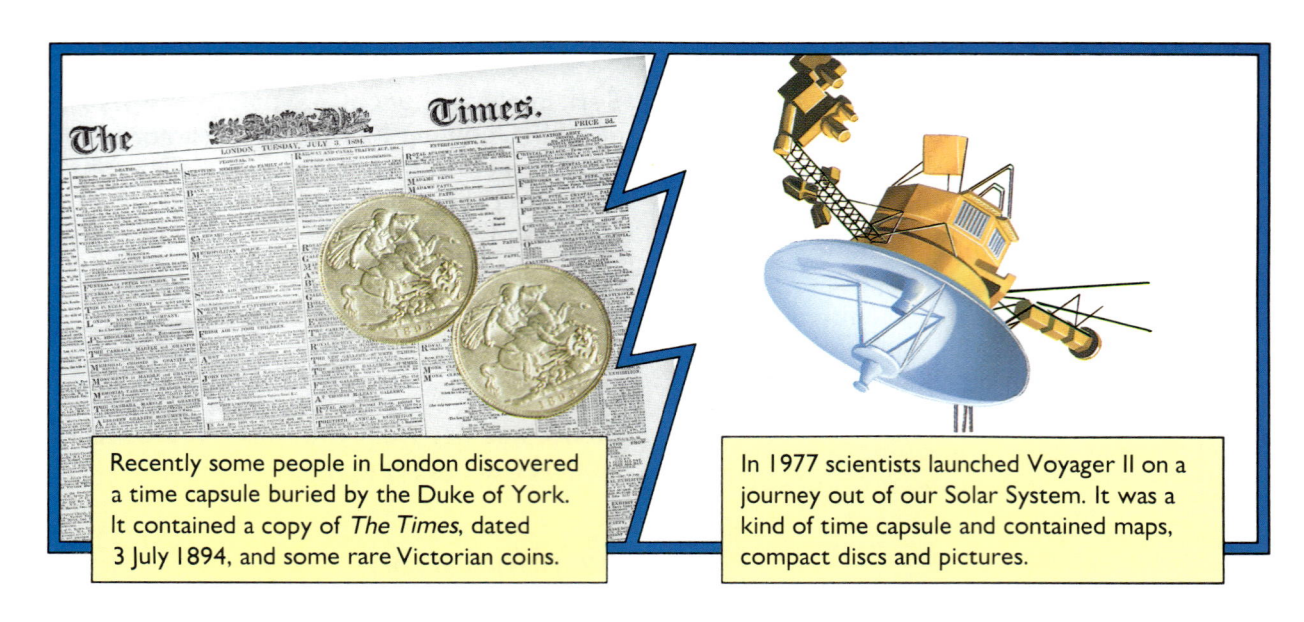

Recently some people in London discovered a time capsule buried by the Duke of York. It contained a copy of *The Times*, dated 3 July 1894, and some rare Victorian coins.

In 1977 scientists launched Voyager II on a journey out of our Solar System. It was a kind of time capsule and contained maps, compact discs and pictures.

A

A time capsule is a container which is buried or sent into space for future generations or aliens to find. In pairs, select five of these objects that you would put into a time capsule to represent our civilisation. Would you include any other objects?

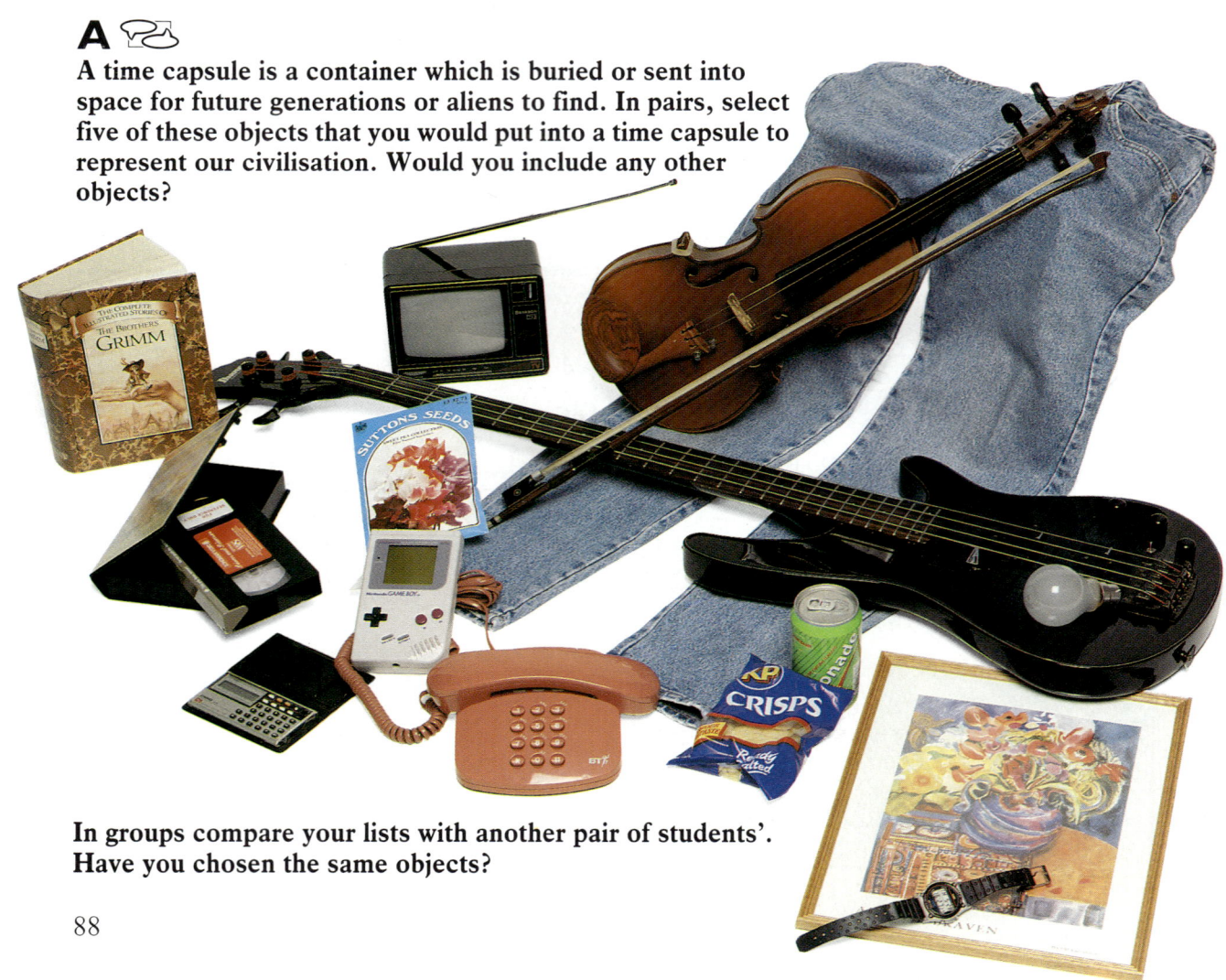

In groups compare your lists with another pair of students'. Have you chosen the same objects?

88

B
Listen to Helen and Peter. Which objects would they take with them if they travelled into the future? Copy and complete the table.

Helen	Peter

Language focus: CONDITIONAL SENTENCES (2)

C
Listen again and match the two parts of the sentences.

1 If you could travel into the future,
2 What would you do
3 If I met an alien,
4 If you could travel into the past,
5 If I were you,
6 If I went there,

a) if you met an alien?
b) I would walk through Athens.
c) what would you take with you?
d) I'd stop talking.
e) I'd try to be friendly.
f) what time would you choose?

D
Look at the sentence in the box. Is the situation really likely or just imaginary? Which tense do we use for the condition and which for the consequence?

Condition	Consequence
If I made a time capsule,	I would put in a newspaper.

E
In pairs, ask about the situations below and give full answers.

Example: A: What would you do if you found a time capsule?
B: If I found a time capsule, I'd take it to a museum.

1 What / do / find time capsule?
2 What / do / meet an alien?
3 Where / go / can travel to any time in the past?
4 Who / meet / can meet anyone you wanted?
5 What / say / meet him/her?
6 What / do / be invisible?
7 Where / go / can travel anywhere in the world now?

F
Which objects from exercise A would you take to the past? Write two sentences.

Example: I would take the calculator because it would help the people who lived then to study mathematics.

Pronunciation

G
Listen to the different ways you can pronounce the letter 'a'.

Group 1
/ɑː/ plant

Group 2
/æ/ travel

Group 3
/eɪ/ take

Group 4
/e/ any

Group 5
/ɔː/ called

Now listen and put the words into the correct group. Then find two words to add to each group.

H
In pairs, play a game. Student A says a word with the letter 'a', student B says a word with the same 'a' sound.

Example: A: planet
B: gravity

42 Revision

Listening

A

Listen to the telephone horoscope. Make notes about your own zodiac sign about these topics:

- family
- love
- money
- lucky number

Dial-a-horoscope
523 1234

Speaking

B

Prediction game. In pairs, take turns to make optimistic predictions. Give pessimistic replies.

Example: A: I think people will live on Mars in the next century.
B: I don't think we'll live on any other planets.
B: I think we will save the Amazon rainforest.
A: I don't. I think we'll destroy it.

How many predictions can you make in five minutes?

C

Think of five surprising or unusual situations.

Examples: 1 An alien walks into the classroom
2 You win a million pounds

In groups, ask other students questions. They imagine what they would do.

Example: A: What would you do if an alien walked into the classroom?
B: I would say hello.
C: I would hide under my desk.
D: I would . . .

Language revision

D

Change these sentences from active to passive.

1 They launch rockets from Cape Canaveral.
2 Cosmonauts do experiments on space stations.
3 They recycle glass.
4 Thick clouds cover Venus.
5 They teach the new alien language in the space school.

E

Match the sentences on the left with the tenses on the right.

1 There'll be 'Moon cities' in the year 3000.
2 I was having lunch at 3 o'clock.
3 I had never seen anything like it before.
4 They are going to build a colony.
5 I saw her yesterday.
6 I have just finished it.
7 She lives in New York.
8 They are destroying the ozone layer.

a) Present simple
b) Present continuous
c) Past simple
d) Past continuous
e) Past perfect
f) Future (*will*)
g) Future (*going to*)
h) Present perfect

Now write a new sentence for each tense.

Learner training

F LEARN TO LEARN

Copy and complete the table.

Noun	Adjective	Adverb
emotion	. . . . .	emotionally
danger	. . . . .	. . . . .
. . . . .	. . . . .	noisily
. . . . .	. . . . .	beautifully
power	. . . . .	. . . . .

Pronunciation review

G *LEARN TO LEARN*

Which can improve your pronunciation?

1. Record and listen to yourself on cassette.
2. Mark the stress on words in your vocabulary book.
3. When you have to say a difficult sound, think about the position of your tongue and lips.
4. Learn some important phonetic symbols that you can recognise when you look up new words in the mini-dictionary.
5. When you find a word impossible to pronounce, look for an alternative that means the same but is easier to say. (Example: Say *activity*, not *exercise*.)

H

Look through your vocabulary book and find ten words difficult for you to pronounce. In groups, make a group list of the ten most difficult words. Read out your list to the rest of the class. What are the ten words which the class finds most difficult to pronounce? Practise saying the words.

Writing

I

Write a science-fiction story which begins 'We left Earth on . . .'.

Stage 1 Write notes for four paragraphs, like this:
 – leaving Earth
 – life on the spaceship (zero-gravity, routine)
 – exploring another planet (meeting aliens)
 – returning to Earth
Stage 2 Write sentences from your notes and try to join sentences with linking words from Lesson 33.
Stage 3 Check verb tenses and spelling.
Stage 4 Give the story a title.

J

Now look at the Module Check on page 107.

Language check

TALKING ABOUT THE FUTURE

We **might** meet aliens one day.
We **may** use suspended animation in space travel.
We **will** land on another planet.
We **won't** travel at the speed of light.

PRESENT PASSIVE

Our food **is grown** in the colony.
Spaceships **are manufactured** by robots.
Everything **is recycled** and nothing **is wasted**.

CONDITIONAL SENTENCES (2)

What **would** you **do** if you **met** an alien?
If I **met** an alien, **I'd try** to be friendly.
If you **could** travel into the past, what time **would** you **choose**?
If I **were** you, **I'd stop** talking.

MODULE 7
SCHOOL 43 Lessons

A

In lessons, do you ever:

- feel bored?
- take notes?
- whisper to other students?
- work hard?
- yawn?

There's not a lot you can find to say about the amoeba. But old Duckpond, standing there in his scruffy jacket, is giving the amoeba all he's got. I think I might die of boredom.

The air smells of rubber, sandwiches and old socks. Nobody seems to be working very hard except boring Lucy Miller who is making copious notes.

Wellington turns round to me and whispers. Duckpond glares. Wellington bends studiously over his book.

Leaning back, Samantha yawns. I watch her little fingertips going delicately to her mouth. And then she stops and sits upright. We all do.

The door opens slowly.

He stops and smiles sweetly round at everyone.

'Hi,' he says. 'I'm Zak.'

B
Read the text and answer the questions.

1. What is the lesson about?
2. What do the pupils call the teacher?
3. Which pupil shows interest in the lesson?
4. Who enters the classroom?
5. Who do you think Zak is?

C
Read the text again and match the adverbs with the definitions.

1. hard
2. studiously
3. delicately
4. slowly
5. sweetly

a) gently, carefully
b) pleasantly, delightfully
c) not fast
d) deliberately, with interest
e) with a lot of effort

D
Choose the answer with the same meaning as the words in *italics*.

1. ... who is *making copious notes*
   a) making a few notes
   b) copying notes
   c) writing lots of notes
2. Duckpond *glares*.
   a) points
   b) looks hard
   c) shouts
3. ... and *sits upright*.
   a) sits down
   b) sits up straight
   c) sits up and turns right

E
Write down all the lessons you have in school and give each a mark out of ten.

Example: History, 9 – I like it a lot.
Science, 3 – I'm not interested.

F
In groups, add up the scores from exercise E and work out the most popular and least popular lessons for your group. Tell the class. Does the rest of the class agree with your group?

Example: Our most popular subject is geography.
The least popular is mathematics.

G
In groups, think of some subjects you would like to study which are *not* on your timetable. Tell the class.

Example: We'd like to do cookery.

Did you know?
Before 1850, girls who went to school only learned music, drawing, dancing and French. Teachers believed this was all they needed to be 'ladies'.

44 Monk on the run

MONK ON THE RUN

1   It's a hot, clear Sunday morning in Kenya's Western Highlands. At the end of a track in the town of Iten the boys of St Patrick's High School are making the most of their free hour between schoolwork and lunch. Some are lying in the sun watching a game of football, others are on the basketball court taking it in turns to aim the ball into a ragged net. Some are working out in the outdoor gym behind the classrooms.

The headteacher, Brother Colm O'Connell, pauses on his walk around the school. 'Now there's a boy to watch – Wilson Kipketer. He's already world class for his age and soon he could be ready to take on anyone.' He knows what he's talking about. Over the years, St Patrick's has produced many top athletes – and all trained by Brother Colm.

When O'Connell arrived in 1976, he knew nothing about athletics. Now he chooses about sixty a year to train seriously – they get up at 5 am and fit their training around their academic work.

'We're a very poor school. We've got very little equipment and we're always short of running shoes,' says O'Connell. 'But we improvise – what we don't have we try to make ourselves.'

Kenya has a good record in the Olympics, and most of their successful athletes are St Patrick's boys. 'After the 1988 Olympics, the Kenyans seemed like a breath of fresh air. They ran naturally and their talent had nothing to do with drugs,' O'Connell explains. 'Suddenly everyone wanted to know Kenya's secret.'

So what is the secret? 'I don't really have a training programme,' says O'Connell. 'If you push someone too hard you can kill his interest. Here the boys run for pleasure, and there's nothing as sophisticated as a starter's gun in this school. And it's true what they say about success – 10% inspiration and 90% perspiration!'

A
Read about St Patrick's school and match these titles with the correct paragraph.

- The Secret of Success
- Kenya's Olympic Success
- The Head Trainer
- Facilities
- Free Time
- Training

B
Now answer the questions.

1. Where is the school?
2. Why is it famous?
3. Who trains the athletes?
4. What time do the best athletes get up?
5. Why did people show interest in Kenya's athletes after 1988?

C

Find these words in the text. Both definitions are possible, but choose the one that is correct in the context.

1 to work out (line 10)
 a) to find a solution to a problem
 b) to do physical exercise
2 brother (line 12)
 a) son of the same parents
 b) member of a religious group
3 to take on (line 16)
 a) to give a job to someone
 b) to oppose someone in a game
4 programme (line 39)
 a) plan of events
 b) an item on television

Language focus: SOME/ANY/NO/EVERY

D

Copy and complete the table.

1	2	3
something	..... /	.....
.....	anyone / anybody	.....
.....	..... /	nowhere
.....	everyone / everybody	.....

Which column do we use for people / activities / places / objects?

E

Look at these sentences about St Patrick's. Rewrite them using words from the table.

Example: 1 *Nobody* works on Sundays between schoolwork and lunch.

1 None of the boys works on Sundays between schoolwork and lunch.
2 O'Connell thinks Wilson Kipketer will do well in the Olympics.
 He thinks Kipketer is ..... to watch.
3 O'Connell thinks Kipketer is the best runner.
 He thinks Kipketer can probably beat ......
4 In 1976, did O'Connell know much about athletics?
 In 1976, did he know ..... about athletics?

F

In pairs, take turns to be a parent who wants to send her/his child to the school. Student A looks at number 4 on page 109 and Student B looks at number 4 on page 111. Use the cues to ask the headteacher questions.

Example: Does everybody learn a foreign language?

- everybody / learn a foreign language?
- anybody / teach computer studies?
- anything / to do at lunchtime?
- anybody / teach music?
- anywhere / to do private study?
- everybody / study science?

School project

G

In pairs, write about your school, like this:

ANGRY COLUMN!
There's nothing to do at lunchtime! Somebody should organise some games because everybody likes sport. There's nowhere to go after school! Somebody should organise a disco because everybody likes music and dancing.

45 Excuses

Late again Blenkinsopp?
What's the excuse this time?
Not my fault sir.
*Who's fault is it then?
Grandma's sir.
Grandma's? What did she do?
She died sir.
Died?
She's seriously dead alright sir.
That makes four grandmothers this term
    Blenkinsopp
And all on P.E. days.
I know. It's very upsetting sir.
How many grandmothers have you got
    Blenkinsopp?
Grandmothers sir? None sir.
You said you had four.
All dead sir.
And what about yesterday Blenkinsopp?
What about yesterday sir?
You were absent yesterday.

That was the dentist sir.
The dentist died?
No sir. My teeth sir.
You missed the maths test Blenkinsopp!
I'd been looking forward to it sir.
Right, line up for P.E.
Can't sir.
No such word as 'can't' Blenkinsopp.
No kit sir.
Where is it?
Home sir.
What's it doing at home?
Not ironed sir.
Couldn't you iron it?
Can't sir.
Why not?
Bad hand sir.
Who usually does it?
Grandma sir.
Why couldn't she do it?
Dead sir.

*Should read 'Whose'

A

Read and listen to the poem and then answer the questions.

1 Which two lessons does Blenkinsopp *not* like?
2 What excuses does Blenkinsopp give for:
   a) being late for P.E.?
   b) missing the mathematics test?
   c) not having his P.E. kit?
3 How many times has he used the same excuse about his grandmother?
4 Do you think Blenkinsopp likes school?

Pronunciation

B

Listen to the poem again. Mark the intonation at the end of the questions.

Example: Whose fault is it then?

Grandma's?

Which questions show surprise or disbelief? Which are *real* questions that need an answer? What do you notice about the intonation?

C

In pairs, practise reading the poem aloud. Take turns to be the teacher and Blenkinsopp.

D

In pairs, take turns to be a pupil giving an excuse to a teacher. Student A looks at number 5 on page 109 and Student B looks at number 5 on page 111.

E

In pairs, select your best excuse from exercise D and act it out in front of the class. When everybody has acted out a dialogue, the class votes for the best excuse.

School project

F

In pairs, make up a questionnaire called 'How To Be A Teacher's Pet'. Write questions, then give them to another pair to answer.

HOW TO BE A TEACHER'S PET

1. When the teacher enters the class, do you:
   a) continue talking to your friend? (0 points)
   b) open your books and smile? (5 points)
   c) wait until the teacher tells you what to do? (3 points)

2. When you see a teacher in the corridor, do you:
   a) say hello? (3 points)
   b) ignore him/her? (0 points)
   c) shake his/her hand and give him/her a sweet? (3 points)

3. When you have a games lesson, do you:
   a) always bring a clean, ironed PE kit? (5 points)
   b) usually bring your kit? (3 points)
   c) make up an excuse not to do games? (0 points)

POINTS

0-3   You are a bad student! You are always in trouble!
4-10 Your behaviour is OK but you'll never be a teacher's pet.
11-15 What a creep! You must be teacher's pet!

Did you know?

Years ago, children used to get prizes if they were never absent from school.

46 Rules

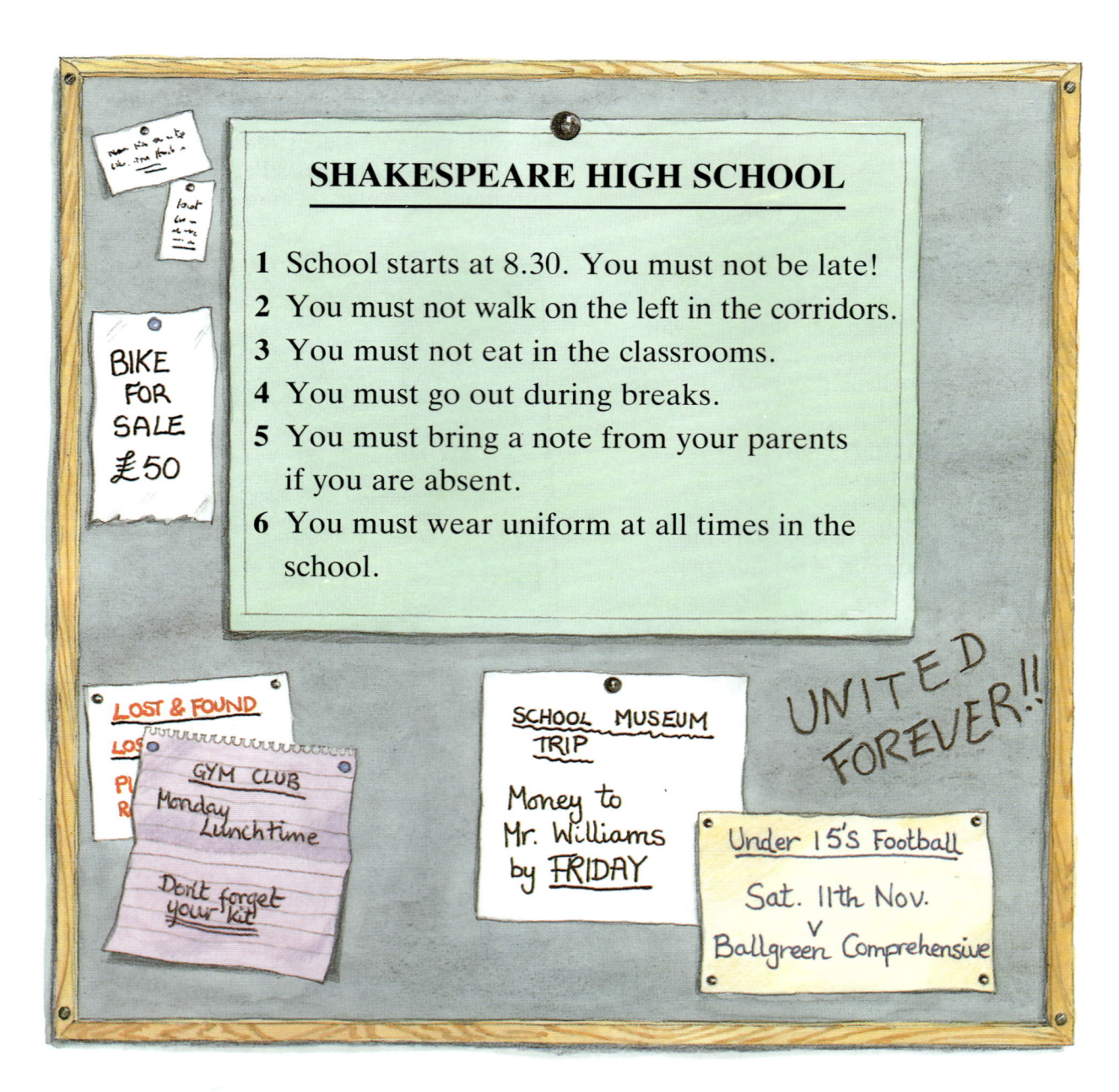

SHAKESPEARE HIGH SCHOOL

1. School starts at 8.30. You must not be late!
2. You must not walk on the left in the corridors.
3. You must not eat in the classrooms.
4. You must go out during breaks.
5. You must bring a note from your parents if you are absent.
6. You must wear uniform at all times in the school.

BIKE FOR SALE £50

LOST & FOUND

GYM CLUB
Monday Lunchtime
Don't forget your kit

SCHOOL MUSEUM TRIP
Money to Mr. Williams by FRIDAY

UNITED FOREVER!!

Under 15's Football
Sat. 11th Nov.
v
Ballgreen Comprehensive

A
In pairs, read the school rules. Do you think they are reasonable?

B
Listen to Debbie talking about Shakespeare High School. Which of the rules does she mention?

Did you know?
In 1911, children went on strike in Britain to protest against the use of the cane.

Language focus: OBLIGATION AND PERMISSION

C
Listen again and complete the sentences with the words below.

must / mustn't / can / don't have to / needn't / should / have to / ought to / let / allowed to / got to

1 You aren't ..... stay in during breaks.
2 You ..... complain.
3 We ..... walk on the right.
4 They don't ..... you wear anything of your own.
5 You ..... wear your uniform at all times.
6 We ..... wear a uniform.
7 We ..... wear what we want.
8 We've ..... be there before 8.30.
9 You ..... be late.
10 We ..... be there till 9 o'clock.
11 You ..... change schools.

D
Which of the verbs in exercise C express:

- Advice? • Obligation? • No obligation? • Prohibition?
- Permission?

Example: should and ought to = Advice

E
Copy and complete the tables for these verbs which express permission.

Affirmative	He	is allowed to	wear jeans in school.
		can	
Negative	They	..... allowed to	
		.....	
Question		..... you allowed to	wear jeans in school?
		..... you	

Affirmative	They	let us	wear jeans in school.
Negative	They	..... let us	
Question		..... they let you	wear jeans in school?

F
Write at least five sentences about rules at your school. Include one that is false. Try to include a variety of expressions from exercise C.

G
In groups, take turns to read out your rules. The others have to say which rule is false.

School project

H
In pairs, write some rules for your 'perfect school'.

SCHOOL RULES

1. Pupils don't have to wear a uniform.
2. Teachers mustn't give homework.
3. You should do some sport every day.
4. Pupils are allowed to eat chewing gum in class.

47 Pupil profile

A
Eva went to live in Britain two years ago. Read her English report for last year. Was she good or bad in these areas?

- Punctuation
- Spelling
- Vocabulary
- Listening
- Reading
- Grammar

> **Did you know?**
> Children in Britain used to believe that if you put a hair on the palm of your hand, the cane would break!

NAME: Eva Fernandez

AGE: 11

CLASS: 6B

SUBJECT	MARK	EFFORT	TEACHER'S COMMENTS
English	5/10	B	Eva does well in reading and listening tests and always brings a dictionary to class. She tries to speak English and she communicates quite well. However, her written English is a disappointment. Her spelling is extremely bad, although she has a good range of vocabulary. She should check spelling in her dictionary. Her stories are interesting and imaginative, but she must improve her punctuation and grammar.
Mathematics	7/10	C+	Satisfactory progress. Eva shows interest in geometry and she should

100

B
Look at an example of Eva's work last year and this year. Mark her errors, like this:

P (punctuation) / S (spelling) / G (grammar) / T (wrong tense)

Now correct the errors.

Example: we *crash* (line 4), T = we crashed

Grade the errors, like this:

★★★★★ = A really horrible mistake
★★★ = A bad mistake   ★ = Not very bad

Underline any *good things* you see – words, expressions, descriptions.

Eva Fernandez, Class 6B, English Composition

It was a luky day for me I waked up erly and the sun was shinning brightly thrugh the window. my dog freddie came into my bedroom he always make me laugh and I decide to take him for a walk at the park. After I get dress and washed and have my brekfast we went out. I threw a ball and freddie ran madly after it but he didn't came back. then I saw him looking at something and touching it carefully with his paw and nose, so I decided

---

Eva Fernandez, Class 7B, English Composition

It was like a nightmare. We were going to the countryside, my family and I, when we had the most awful experience. As we were driving, we crash into a car. We were hurt, but we continued the jurney. When we got to the country, we explored a deep forest. We found a cave and go in. It was cool, dark and gloomy we lit a candle and by the light of the candle we saw a huge, brown, wild bear! We run and run until we were

---

C
Write a new report on Eva's English writing.

Stage 1 Read last year's report and compare it with the writing you have corrected. Make notes about what has improved, got worse or stayed the same.

Stage 2 Prepare a few sentences. Decide how you can join some using *but*, *however* and *although*.

Stage 3 Write your report and sign it.

D
In pairs, exchange an example of your writing. Look through each other's work and do the same as you did for Eva in exercise B. Prepare some notes about your partner's written English and give him/her a mark out of ten.

E
Talk to your partner about his/her written English. Point out some good things and explain one error. Say the mark you have given. Does your partner agree?

School project

F
The best/worst English student. Write an amusing report.

101

48 Your school

A
Look at the three school plans.

1 Has your school got any of these facilities?
2 Which ones would you like to have?
3 Which facilities would you add to improve these schools?
4 Which school do you prefer?

B
Listen to the three pupils talking about their plans for a perfect school. Match the pupils with the plans.

Language focus: EXPRESSIONS OF LOCATION

C
Put a word or phrase from the box into the sentences.

next to	between	at the end of	opposite
facing	surrounded by	in the corner	
in the centre of	around	beside	

1 School 1 has a teacher's room . . . . . the two playgrounds.
2 In school 2, the swimming pool is . . . . . gardens.
3 School 2's music room is . . . . . the drama room.
4 In school 1, the bicycles are . . . . . a play area.
5 In school 1, if you go in entrance B, the video room is . . . . . the corridor on the left.
6 There is a shop . . . . . the coffee bar in school 1.
7 There is a big play area . . . . . of school 3.
8 The restaurant is . . . . . the teachers' entrance in school 1.
9 There are some studios . . . . . of the music room in school 3.
10 Schools 2 and 3 have an athletics track . . . . . the football field.

D
Are these sentences true or false? Correct the false ones.

Example: Sentence 1 = False. It's opposite the art room.

1 In school 1, the library is opposite the computer room.
2 In school 1, if you go in entrance A, the coffee bar is at the end of the corridor.
3 In school 2, the games room is facing the coffee bar.
4 In school 1, the video room is beside the library.
5 The play area in school 3 is surrounded by classrooms.

Helen

Steve

Brian

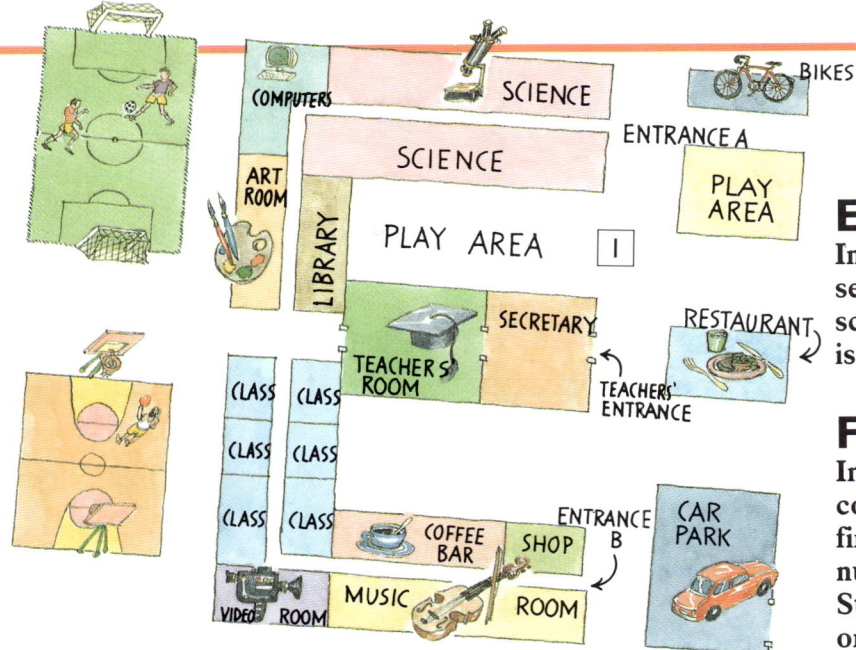

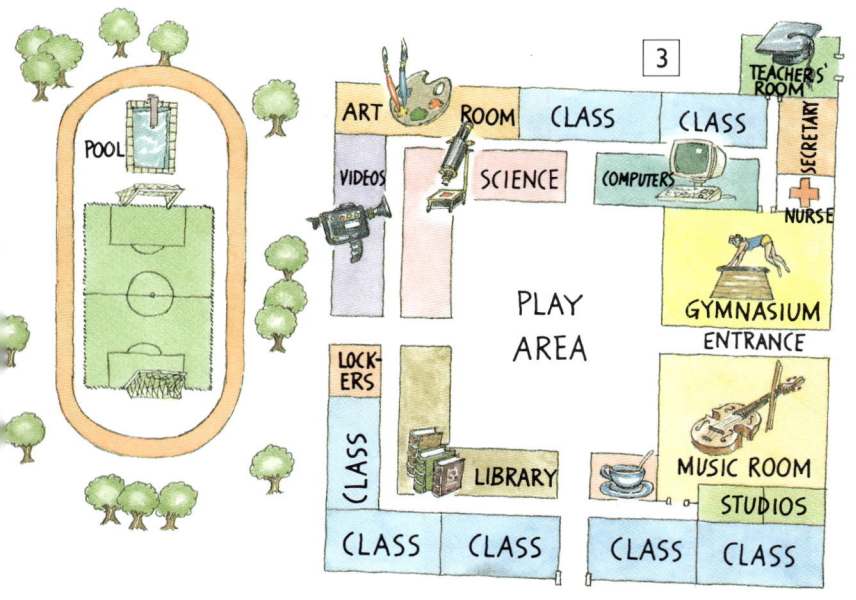

E

In groups, take turns to say a sentence about one of the schools. The others say if it is true or false.

F

In pairs, see who can complete the school plan first. Student A looks at number 6 on page 109 and Student B looks at number 6 on page 111.

Example: A: Is the computer room next to the coffee bar?
B: No, it isn't.

School project

G

Draw a plan of your own perfect school and label the facilities.

Pronunciation

H

Listen to some of the different ways you can pronounce the letter 'e'.

Group 1   *Group 2*
/e/ lesson   /ə/ whisper

Group 3   *Group 4*
/ɪ/ before   /i:/ he

Group 5
/ /played (no sound!)

Listen to these words and put them in the correct group. Can you find more words from this module to put in each group?

103

49 Revision

Listening

A

Listen to the three dialogues.

1 What did the pupils do wrong?
2 What is his/her excuse?
3 Do you believe the pupils?

Speaking

B

Look at the notes you made on another student's English in Lesson 47. In pairs, take turns to be the English teacher giving advice.

Example: You *should* revise the grammar. You *needn't* worry about your spelling – it's very good.

C

In groups, take turns to say a sentence about your school. The others say if it's true or false.

Example: The headteacher's room is *next to* the secretary's office.

Language revision

D

Look at the Language focus in Lessons 44, 46 and 48. Then fill in the gaps.

1 Does . . . . . teach music in your school?
2 There's a computer . . . . . our classroom.
3 Do you . . . . . to do a foreign language in your school?
4 There's . . . . . to do at lunchtimes – we get bored.
5 The play area is . . . . . trees.
6 . . . . . broke a window in our classroom.
7 Everybody . . . . . do science in our school.
8 The headteacher's office is . . . . . the main corridor.
9 You . . . . . go to school after the age of 16 if you don't want to.
10 We . . . . . eat or chew gum in class.

Learner training

E

Below are some words from this module. Copy and complete the table. You can use the mini-dictionary.

Noun	Verb	Adjective	Adverb
. . . . .	. . . . .	bored	–
. . . . .	. . . . .	. . . . .	studiously
. . . . .	succeed	successful	. . . . .
. . . . .	deepen	deep	. . . . .
. . . . .	horrify	horrible	. . . . .
. . . . .	–	disastrous	. . . . .

F

Look at the sentences. Match the numbers with the words in the list below.

Verb / Pronoun / Noun / Adverb / Adjective / Article

1	2	3	4	5	6
He	trains	the	Kenyan	athletes	hard.

1	2	3	4	5	6
She	drank	the	hot	coffee	slowly.

Now put these words in the correct order to make a sentence.

did / difficult / they / carefully / housework / the

School project

G

In groups of four, invent a new school.

Stage 1 Collect the writing you have done in this module and choose the best timetable, school rules, complaints, teacher's pet questionnaire, pupil profile and plan of the school.

Stage 2 Discuss the following aspects of your invented school – name, location, number of students, special facilities, interesting people, your opinion about it.

Stage 3 Divide the work between you. Each person writes about one aspect of the school.

Stage 4 Check each other's work for mistakes and make suggestions to improve it.

Stage 5 Write the work neatly and display it on the wall or in a folder. Show it to other students.

H

Now do the End-of-year self-evaluation on page 106.

Language check

SOME-, ANY-, NO-, EVERY-

Has **anybody** seen my pen? I've looked **everywhere** but I can't find it. I think **somebody** has taken it.
This town's boring. There's **nothing** to do and **nowhere** to go.

OBLIGATION AND PERMISSION

Children **must** go to school until they are 16. After that they **don't have to**.
You **should/ought to** pay attention in class.
We **have to** wear a uniform.
They **let** us go home early on Fridays.
We aren't **allowed to** eat in the classrooms.
You **needn't** wait for me – I'll be very late.
You **mustn't** forget your games kit.
We **can** cycle to school if we want.

EXPRESSIONS OF LOCATION

The library is **facing/opposite** the video room.
Our school is **in the centre of** the city.
Their school is **surrounded by** trees. Lots of trees are **around it**.
My room is **at the end of** the main corridor.
I usually sit **in the corner**, **next to** Helen. I sit **beside** her.
The teacher's desk is **between** us and the blackboard.

End-of-year self-evaluation

Grade yourself in the following way:
- [A] I have no problems.
- [B] I sometimes have difficulties.
- [C] I have a lot of problems with this.

Speaking
- [ ] Talking about yourself – personal information, family, hobbies, etc.
- [ ] Telling stories
- [ ] Expressing opinions – saying what you think
- [ ] Using English in the class – asking for things, giving excuses
- [ ] Describing people
- [ ] Describing places
- [ ] Using English outside the class – shops, on the phone, to tourists

Writing
- [ ] a formal letter
- [ ] instructions
- [ ] paragraph plans
- [ ] Checking and editing
- [ ] a postcard
- [ ] a story
- [ ] notes
- [ ] a poem

Reading (texts in this book)
- [ ] magazine articles
- [ ] stories
- [ ] information texts, e.g. encyclopedia
- [ ] letters
- [ ] poems

Listening
- [ ] to your teacher
- [ ] to stories (on the cassette)
- [ ] to dialogues/conversations (on the cassette)
- [ ] to radio programmes (on the cassette)

Grammar
- [ ] Comparative and superlative adjectives
- [ ] Past simple
- [ ] Past continuous
- [ ] Past perfect
- [ ] Question tags
- [ ] Passives
- [ ] Relative pronouns
- [ ] Conditional sentences
- [ ] Modal verbs (*must*, *should*, *can*, etc.)
- [ ] Present perfect
- [ ] *Used to*
- [ ] Future
- [ ] Prepositions

Now write an 'end of year' report on your English, like the report in Lesson 47. See if your teacher agrees!
Good luck next year!

Module check

Do this after each module. Do numbers 1 to 4 and discuss the answers with your partner. Then do numbers 5 and 6 on your own. Write the answers in your notebook.

1
Which was your favourite lesson in the module you've just done? Why?

Example: Champions because I like football.

2
Write down two interesting or unusual facts from the module you've just done.

Example: White sharks can bite through metal.
Vampire bats have got twenty-two teeth.

3
Look back through the module. Which two exercises were very difficult for you?

Example: Lesson 10, exercise A – listening to the story
Lesson 12, exercise A – reading the texts

4
Look at the structures in the Language check in the Revision lesson. Find the lessons where the structures occur.

Example: Lesson 2 – *still, yet, already*

Give yourself a mark for each structure, like this:

5 – I have no problems with it and I never make mistakes.
4 – I only make mistakes occasionally.
3 – I sometimes have problems with it.
2 – I don't understand it very well and I often make mistakes.
1 – I don't understand it!

Example: Present perfect with *still/yet/already* – 2
Comparatives – 4
Future, *going to*/present continuous – 3

5
Look at the *Test yourself* exercise for this module in the Activity Book. Do the exercise and then correct it using the answers at the back of the book. Write down your score.

6
Look at the *Useful vocabulary* section in the Activity Book. Check you have the words in your own vocabulary book.

PAIRWORK ACTIVITIES A

1
Read about the Aztecs and make notes. Your partner is going to ask you questions.

The Aztecs built a great empire in Mexico in the 15th century. Their capital, Tenochtitlan, was bigger than any city in Europe at the time. They built it on an island in a great lake. The Aztecs didn't have transport with wheels and carried all their heavy things around in boats, travelling along canals. The poor people ate cereals and beans, and sometimes rabbits and dogs. An omelette cooked with baby frogs was a special meal. Turtles were delicacies for rich people. The Aztecs discovered how to make rubber balls, and played a game very similar to modern basketball. All Aztec boys, at the age of eight, learned how to fight. The main weapons were spears and wooden clubs with sharp pieces of glass stuck into them.

2
Look at the question cues below and ask your partner questions. The answers are in brackets.

Example: Who / fight / against the Spanish in South America? (Bolivar)
Who fought against the Spanish in South America?

a) Who / build / the Pyramids? (The Ancient Egyptians)
b) Who / write / *A Tale of Two Cities*? (Charles Dickens)
c) Who / write / *Romeo and Juliet*? (Shakespeare)
d) Who / paint / *Guernica*? (Picasso)
e) Who / go / to America in 1492? (Columbus)
f) Who / have / the *Golden Touch*? (King Midas)
g) Who / sing / *Yesterday*? (The Beatles)
h) Who / make / the record album *Thriller*? (Michael Jackson)
i) Who / win / the 1986 World Cup? (Argentina)
j) Who / invent / the telephone? (Alexander Bell)

Now answer your partner's questions.

3
Tell your partner you have:

- been to Machu Picchu
- been to the Moon
- written a song with Paul McCartney
- driven a Rolls-Royce

PAIRWORK ACTIVITIES

4
You are the headteacher of this school. Read the information and then answer your partner's questions.

All pupils study mathematics, science and a foreign language – some choose English, some French and some German. Pupils get a lot of homework every day, but not at weekends. The school is also closed at weekends. Children have an hour and a half for lunch, and during this time they can study in the library or join a music club – there is a very good music teacher at the school. The school is in the centre of the city, and unfortunately there is nowhere to play sport – in games lessons, students have to go to a sports centre by bus. The school is near to public transport and pupils can't come to school on bicycles or motorbikes.

5
You are the teacher. Ask your partner these questions and interrogate him/her.

- Why were you talking in class?
- Why haven't you done your homework?
- Why did you walk out of the class?
- Where is your pen?

Now you are a pupil. You did the following things. Prepare some good excuses!

- You were eating in class.
- You were looking out of the window.
- You were absent from school yesterday.
- You copied in the mathematics exam.

6
Look at the plan below. Ask your partner questions to find out where these rooms are:

- coffee bar
- gymnasium
- computer room
- library
- nurse's room

Also answer your partner's questions. If you find out where all the rooms are before your partner, you are the winner.

Swimming Pool	Games Room	Video Room	Music Room	Maths Room
G A R D E N S		Geography Room	History Room	English Room
		Art Room		Drama Room
Secretary's Office	Toilets	Teachers' Room	Reception Area	Science Lab
Play Area		Lockers		

109

B

1
Read about the Vikings and make notes. Your partner is going to ask you questions.

The Vikings originally came from Scandinavia, but in the 9th and 10th centuries they travelled to many lands including most of Europe as far as Russia and Turkey, and south as far as Spain. They sailed in long wooden boats, and some people think they reached North America. Vikings were violent people, and fought with iron swords and spears. At home, however, most Vikings were simple farmers. A typical meal was boiled meat and vegetables with a type of beer. In their free time Vikings enjoyed playing a board game similar to chess, and they also organised horse races.

2
Answer your partner's questions. Then look at the question cues below and ask your partner questions. The answers are in brackets.

Example: Who / fight / against the Spanish in South America? (Bolivar)
Who fought against the Spanish in South America?

a) Who / build / the *Great Wall*? (The Ancient Chinese)
b) Who / paint / *La Giaconda*? (Leonardo da Vinci)
c) Who / have / hair made of snakes? (Medusa)
d) Who / write / *Animal Farm*? (George Orwell)
e) Who / invent / the electric light bulb? (Thomas Edison)
f) Who / write / *Hamlet*? (Shakespeare)
g) Who / go / to the moon in 1969? (Neil Armstrong or Buzz Aldrin)
h) Who / win / the 1990 World Cup? (Germany)
i) Who / sing / the song *My Way*? (Frank Sinatra)
j) Who / make / the record album *Like a Virgin*? (Madonna)

3
Tell your partner you have:

- seen the Pyramids in Egypt
- been to Disneyworld
- played tennis with Boris Becker
- flown in Concorde

PAIRWORK ACTIVITIES

4
You are the headteacher of this school. Read the information and then answer your partner's questions.

The school has excellent sports facilities – basketball courts, tennis courts, a modern gymnasium and football and hockey fields. Children in the school are aged from 6 to 16 years old. Only those pupils over 11 get homework. Everybody in the school takes maths, English and science. Children can eat lunch in the school and one of the teachers organises a lunchtime discotheque in the hall. There is no library or music room in the school. The school is open on Saturdays for sports activities. The school organises school buses, and nobody can come to school by bicycle.

5
You are a pupil. You did the following things. Prepare some good excuses!

- You were talking in class.
- You haven't done your homework.
- You walked out of the class.
- You haven't got a pen.

Now you are the teacher. Ask your partner these questions and interrogate him/her.

- Why were you eating in class?
- Why were you looking out of the window?
- Why were you absent yesterday?
- Why did you copy in the mathematics exam?

6
Look at the plan below. Answer your partner's questions. Ask your partner questions to find out where these places are:

- art room
- science lab
- swimming pool
- music room
- secretary's office

If you find out where all the rooms are before your partner, you are the winner.

	Games Room	Video Room		Maths Room
G A R D E N S	Computer Room	Geography Room	History Room	English Room
	Library		Coffee Bar	Drama Room
	Toilets	Teachers' Room	Reception Area	
Play Area	Gymnasium	Lockers		Nurse

111

Irregular verb list

bite	bit	bitten	sing	sang	sung
break	broke	broken	sink	sank	sunk
bring	brought	brought	sit	sat	sat
build	built	built	sleep	slept	slept
buy	bought	bought	speak	spoke	spoken
catch	caught	caught	spell	spelt	spelt
choose	chose	chosen	spend	spent	spent
come	came	come	stand	stood	stood
cost	cost	cost	stick	stuck	stuck
cut	cut	cut	swim	swam	swum
do	did	done	take	took	taken
draw	drew	drawn	teach	taught	taught
drink	drank	drunk	tell	told	told
drive	drove	driven	think	thought	thought
eat	ate	eaten	understand	understood	understood
fall	fell	fallen	wake (up)	woke/waked	woken/waked (up)
feed	fed	fed	wear	wore	worn
feel	felt	felt	win	won	won
find	found	found	write	wrote	written
get	got	got			
give	gave	given			
go	went	gone			
grow	grew	grown			
have	had	had			
hear	heard	heard			
hide	hid	hidden/hid			
hit	hit	hit			
hold	held	held			
hurt	hurt	hurt			
keep	kept	kept			
know	knew	known			
lay	laid	laid			
learn	learnt/learned	learnt/learned			
leave	left	left			
lose	lost	lost			
make	made	made			
mean	meant	meant			
meet	met	met			
pay	paid	paid			
put	put	put			
read	read	read			
ride	rode	ridden			
ring	rang	rung			
run	ran	run			
say	said	said			
see	saw	seen			
shoot	shot	shot			
show	showed	shown/showed			

Phonetic chart

CONSONANTS

symbol	key word
/p/	pen
/b/	back
/t/	tea
/d/	day
/k/	key
/g/	get
/tʃ/	cheer
/dʒ/	jump
/f/	fat
/v/	view
/θ/	thing
/ð/	then
/s/	soon
/z/	zero
/ʃ/	fish
/ʒ/	pleasure
/h/	hot
/m/	come
/n/	sun
/ŋ/	sung
/l/	led
/r/	red
/j/	yet
/w/	wet

VOWEL

symbol	key word
/i:/	sheep
/ɪ/	ship
/e/	bed
/æ/	bad
/ɑ:/	calm
/ɒ/	pot
/ɔ:/	saw
/ʊ/	put
/u:/	boot
/ʌ/	cut
/ɜ:/	bird
/ə/	China

DIPHTHONGS

symbol	key word
/eɪ/	make
/əʊ/	note
/aɪ/	bite
/aʊ/	now
/ɔɪ/	boy
/ɪə/	here
/eə/	there
/ʊə/	tour

Mini-dictionary

This mini-dictionary will help you to understand all the words that are *either* important to remember *or* necessary to do the activities. Remember that you don't have to understand every word when you read a text. If you find a word in one of the texts which is not in the mini-dictionary then that word is not essential to do the activity.

The definitions in this mini-dictionary are taken from the **Longman New Junior English Dictionary** (first published 1984).

We recommend that you refer to this dictionary for words not included here. Remember that this mini-dictionary is not a substitute for a complete dictionary.

A

absent /'æbsənt/ *adjective* not there; not present: *He was* **absent** *from work last Tuesday.*
achieve /ə'tʃi:v/ *verb (present participle* **achieving**, *past* **achieved**) to do or get successfully by working: *He* **achieved** *top marks in the examination.* **achievement** *noun* something that you have worked hard for
aerosol /'eərəspl/ *noun* a small container for liquids such as paint, perfume, etc., which are forced out as a spray when you press a button
afraid /ə'freɪd/ *adjective* frightened: *James says he's not* **afraid** *of lions!*
age /eɪdʒ/ *noun* 1 the amount of time someone has lived or something has been: *What is the* **age** *of that church? Mary is eight years* **of age**. 2 a period of time in history: *the Iron* **Age** 3 (*often plural*) a long time: *I haven't seen her* **for ages**.
albino /æl'bi:nəʊ/ *noun* a person or animal with very light skin and hair and pink eyes
alien /'eɪliən/ *noun* a creature from another planet
alongside /ə,lɒŋ'saɪd/ *preposition, adverb* by the side of: *Put your chair* **alongside** *mine.*
amoeba /ə'mi:bə/ *noun (plural* **amoebas** *or* **amoebae**) a very small creature which lives in water
analyse /'ænəlaɪz/ *verb (present participle* **analysing**, *past* **analysed**) to find out exactly what something is made of: *The scientist* **analysed** *the milk and found it contained too much water.*
ancient /'eɪnʃənt/ *adjective* very old: *to study* **ancient** *history*
appear /ə'pɪəʳ/ *verb* 1 to seem: *She* **appears** *to be unhappy.* 2 to come into sight suddenly: *Her head* **appeared** *round the door.*

argument /'ɑ:gjʊmənt/ *noun* a disagreement; quarrel
army /'ɑ:mi/ *noun (plural* **armies**) a large number of soldiers fighting together
arrest /ə'rest/ *verb* to make someone a prisoner: *The criminal was* **arrested** *yesterday.*
artificial /,ɑ:tɪ'fɪʃl/ *adjective* not real: **artificial** *flowers*
assassin /ə'sæsɪn/ *noun* a murderer, especially one who kills someone important, such as a president or king
astrology /ə'strɒlədʒi/ *noun (no plural)* the study of the effects of the stars and planets on your character and life
astronaut /'æstrənɔ:t/ *noun* a person who travels in space
astronomy /ə'strɒnəmi/ *noun (no plural)* the study of the sun, moon, and stars
athletics /æθ'letɪks/ *noun (no plural)* the practice of sports such as running, jumping and throwing
atmosphere /'ætməsfɪəʳ/ *noun (no plural)* 1 the air surrounding the Earth and other planets 2 a feeling that a place or group of people give you: *the exciting* **atmosphere** *of a football match*

B

back[1] /bæk/ *noun* 1 the part of the body from the neck to the legs: *The* '**backbone** *runs down the* **back** *from the neck to the middle of the body. You shouldn't talk about Agnes* **behind her back** (= when she's not here). 2 the part that is furthest from the front; at or near the end: *Write this exercise at the* **back** *of your book. There's a hut at the back of* (= behind) *the house. Peter's shirt is* ,1 **back to front** – *he's got the buttons down his* **back**!
back[2] *adverb* 1 at or towards the back part; away from the front: *She tied her long hair* **back** *with a band. Stand* **back** *from the fire; it's very hot.* 2 to or in a place where something or someone was before: *Put the book* **back** *on the shelf when you've finished it.* 3 in return or in reply: *I wrote to her, and she wrote* **back** (*to me*) *the next day.*
bandage[1] /'bændɪdʒ/ *noun* a long piece of cloth used for covering a wound
bandage[2] *verb (present participle* **bandaging**, *past* **bandaged**) to tie a bandage on
bat /bæt/ *noun* 1 a piece of wood used for hitting the ball in some games 2 a small animal that flies at night
battle /'bætl/ *noun* a fight between people, ships or aircraft
beast /bi:st/ *noun* an animal
beautiful /'bju:tɪfəl/ *adjective* very pretty; very pleasing: *What a* **beautiful** *day!* **beautifully** /'bju:tɪfli/ *adverb: The children danced* **beautifully**.
beauty /'bju:ti/ *noun (no plural)* being beautiful: *a flower of great* **beauty**
bee /bi:/ *noun* a stinging, flying insect that makes honey
believe /bɪ'li:v/ *verb (present participle*

believing, *past* **believed**) 1 to think someone is honest, right or true: *Simon says he gave you the money, and I* **believe** *him. The soldiers all* **believe in** *their leader.* 2 to think something is true: *I* **believe** *that he'll do what he said.*
bend /bend/ *verb (past* **bent** /bent/) 1 to make into a curve: *He* **bent** *the wire.* 2 to bend one's body: *She* **bent** (*over*) *to pick up a book from the floor.*
blood /blʌd/ *noun (no plural)* the red liquid that flows round the body
board /bɔ:d/ *verb* to go on board; to get into (ship or vehicle): *He* **boarded** *the bus/plane/ship/train/taxi.*
body /'bɒdi/ *noun (plural* **bodies**) 1 the whole of a person or animal, but not the mind 2 the central part, not the head, arms or legs: *He had a cut on his leg and two more on his* **body**. 3 a dead person or animal
BMX bike /bi: em eks 'baɪk/ *noun* a kind of bicycle with a strong frame and small wheels with thick tyres which can be used on rough ground
bore /bɔ:ʳ/ *verb (present participle* **boring**, *past* **bored**) to make someone tired or uninterested, by something dull: *I'm* **bored** *with this job.* '**boredom** *noun (no plural)* being bored '**boring** *adjective: a* **boring** *job*
bounce /baʊns/ *verb (present participle* **bouncing**, *past* **bounced**) 1 to spring or jump back: *The girls were* **bouncing** *on the bed.* 2 to make something do this: *The children were* **bouncing** *a ball.*
boxing /'bɒksɪŋ/ *noun* a kind of fighting in which you wear gloves and hit the other person with your hands
brave /breɪv/ *adjective* without fear, or not showing it: *a* **brave** *fireman* **bravely** *adverb* **bravery** *noun*
break /breɪk/ *noun* a short rest: *Let's have a* **break**.
breathe /bri:ð/ *verb (present participle* **breathing**, *past* **breathed**) to take air into the body and let it out
breed /bri:d/ *verb (past* **bred** /bred/) 1 to produce young ones: *Some animals will not* **breed** *in cages.* 2 to keep animals so that they will produce young ones: *He* **breeds** *cattle.*
bright /braɪt/ *adjective* 1 sending out light: *The sun was very* **bright**. 2 having a clear colour; not dull: *a* **bright** *yellow dress*
bring /brɪŋ/ *verb (past* **brought** /brɔ:t/) to carry something, or go with someone, to the speaker: *Has anyone* **brought** *a ball to school today? If you take that book home,* **bring** *it* **back** *tomorrow.*
brother /'brʌðəʳ/ *noun* 1 a boy or man with the same parents as another person: *Peter is Mary's* **brother**. 2 a man who lives in a religious community
bucket /'bʌkɪt/ *noun* a metal or plastic container with a handle for holding or carrying water, etc.
bury /'beri/ *verb (present participle* **burying**, *past* **buried** /'berid/) 1 to put a dead person into the ground 2 to put or hide something in the ground: *The dog* **buried** *the bone.*

113

C

cabin /'kæbɪn/ *noun* **1** a room on a ship or aeroplane **2** a small wooden house

cable /'keɪbl/ *noun* **1** a thick rope **2** wires that carry electricity or telephone calls **3** a message sent by cable

cage /keɪdʒ/ *noun* a box with metal bars where birds or animals are kept

campaign /kæm'peɪn/ *noun* a plan to get a result: *a* **campaign** *to stop people smoking*

can /kæn/ *or* **tin** *noun* a container made of metal: *Food in* **cans** *is called* **canned** *food.*

canal /kə'næl/ *noun* a man-made river: *The* **canals** *take water to the rice fields.*

candle /'kændl/ *noun* a long piece of wax with a string in the middle which burns to give light

cane /keɪn/ *noun* a stick used to hit children with

canoe¹ /kə'nuː/ *noun* a narrow, light boat

canoe² *verb* (*present participle* **canoeing**, *past* **canoed**) to travel by canoe: *They* **canoed** *up the river. Let's go* **canoeing** *this weekend!*

career /kə'rɪəʳ/ *noun* a person's working life: *Our teacher gave us some advice about different* **careers***.*

carnival /'kɑːnɪvəl/ *noun* a public procession with music and dancing in celebration of a special occasion or religious holiday

cartoon /kɑː'tuːn/ *noun* **1** a funny drawing **2** a film made by photographing drawings: *a Disney* **cartoon**

catch /kætʃ/ *verb* (*past* **caught** /kɔːt/) **1** to get in the hand and hold: *She threw the ball and I* **caught** *it.* **2** to run after and take hold of: *We ran after the dog and* **caught** *it.* **3** to get: *I* **caught** *the train. She* **caught** *a cold. I walked fast but I couldn't* **catch up with** *you* (= couldn't get to where you were).

century /'sentʃərɪ/ *noun* (*plural* **centuries**) (a period of) one hundred years: *It was built in the 19th* **century***.*

CFC /'siː ef siː/ *noun* short for chlorofluorocarbon; chemical compounds used in manufacturing, in refrigerators and in aerosols, which damage the ozone layer

champion /'tʃæmpɪən/ *noun* someone who is the best at something, especially a game or sport **championship** *noun* a competition to find who is the best at something: *Our team won the swimming* **championships***.*

cheetah /'tʃiːtə/ *noun* a wild animal which is one of the big cats and lives in Africa

childhood /'tʃaɪldhʊd/ *noun* the time when you are a child

claw /klɔː/ *noun* one of the sharp, hard points on the foot of a bird or animal

climb /klaɪm/ *verb* to go up: *The two girls* **climbed** (**up**) *the tree. Let's go* **climbing** *in the Alps.*

close /kləʊs/ *adjective* **1** near: *I live* **close** *to the shops. They were standing* **close together** (= very near each other). **2** liking or loving: *Sarah and Jane are* **close** *friends.*

cloth /klɒθ/ *noun* (*no plural*) a soft substance made of wool, cotton, etc.; material: *She bought some* **cloth** *to make some new dresses.*

clothes /kləʊðz/ *plural noun* things we wear

club /klʌb/ *noun* **1** a group of people who meet for some purpose: *a football* **club** **2** a large heavy stick

coach /kəʊtʃ/ *verb* to give special lessons: *She* **coached** *him for the English examination.*

coal /kəʊl/ *noun* (*no plural*) black hard material dug out of the ground and burnt to give heat

colony /'kɒlənɪ/ *noun* (*plural* **colonies**) a country that is under the control of another country

come /kʌm/ (*present participle* **coming** /'kʌmɪŋ/, *past* **came** /keɪm/, *past participle* **come**) to move towards the person speaking: *"***Come** *here Mary, I want to speak to you!" My shoe has* **come off** (= it is not on my foot any more). *I* **come from** *London* (= I was born there, my home is there). **come across** *verb* to find or meet by chance: *I* **came across** *some old diaries while I was tidying my room.*

come away *verb* to become separated from something: *The handle* **came away** *in my hand.*

come back *verb* to return: *Her parents told her to* **come back** *home before ten o'clock.*

come up *verb* **1** to be discussed: *The question of the new road* **came up** *again at the meeting.* **2** to happen: *I've got to go home – something important has just* **come up***.*

come up to *verb* **1** to come near to someone or something: *A man* **came up** *to me in the street.* **2** to equal: *His performance didn't* **come up** *to his usual standards.*

complain /kəm'pleɪn/ *verb* to say that something is not good, or that you are unhappy or angry with something: *We* **complained about** *the bad food.* **complaint** *noun: We made a* **complaint** *about the food.*

conquer /'kɒŋkəʳ/ *verb* to defeat in war: *to* **conquer** *the enemy*

copious /'kəʊpɪəs/ *adjective* a lot: *She took copious notes of everything we said.*

corridor /'kɒrɪdɔːʳ/ *noun* a long narrow part of a building, with rooms on each side of it: *Go down the* **corridor***, to the third room on the left.*

cosmonaut /'kɒzmənɔːt/ *noun* a Russian astronaut (someone who travels in space)

cotton /'kɒtən/ *noun* (*no plural*) a plant grown in hot countries for the fine white threads (**cotton**) which cover its seeds and which are made into thread or material: *She sewed the* **cotton** *dress with* **cotton** (*thread*).

court /kɔːt/ *noun* an open space where games are played: *a* **'tennis-court**

creative /kriː'eɪtɪv/ *adjective* having a lot of new ideas, and being imaginative or artistic: *She's very* **creative***; she makes all her own clothes.*

creature /'kriːtʃəʳ/ *noun* an animal or insect

crew /kruː/ *noun* the people who work on a ship

crime /kraɪm/ *noun* something that is wrong and can be punished by the law: *Stealing is a* **crime***.*

crop /krɒp/ *noun* **1** food that is grown: *Which* **crops** *does he grow?* **2** vegetables, grain, etc. that are cut or gathered at one time: *a* **crop** *of apples*

crowd /kraʊd/ *noun* a large mass of people: *a* **crowd** (*of people*) *at the football match* **crowded** /'kraʊdɪd/ *adjective* full of people: *I don't like the market; it is too* **crowded***.*

curious /'kjʊərɪəs/ *adjective* **1** wanting to know about things or people: *It is good to be* **curious** *about the world around you.* **2** strange or odd: *a* **curious** *fact*

cut /kʌt/ *verb* (*present participle* **cutting**, *past* **cut**) to break with a knife or blade: *He* **cut** *the apple in half. He has* **cut** *his leg, and it is bleeding. She* **cut** *her hair* (= made it shorter). **Cut down** *the tree* (= cut it so that it falls down). *He was* **cutting up** *the chicken* (= cutting it into pieces).

cycle /'saɪkl/ *verb* (*present participle* **cycling**, *past* **cycled**) to ride a bicycle: *He* **cycles** *to school every day. I enjoy* **cycling***.*

D

damage¹ /'dæmɪdʒ/ *noun* (*no plural*) harm, especially to things

damage² *verb* (*present participle* **damaging**, *past* **damaged**) to hurt; cause damage to: *The cars were badly* **damaged** *in the accident.*

danger /'deɪndʒəʳ/ *noun* **1** (*no plural*) the possibility of loss or harm: *There is always* **danger** (*of floods*) *in a storm. He put his life* **in danger** *when he ran across the busy street.* **2** something that causes danger: *the* **dangers** *of smoking* **dangerous** *adjective: a* **dangerous** *bend in the road* **dangerously** *adverb: We were* **dangerously** *close to the edge of the water.*

dare /deəʳ/ *verb* (*present participle* **daring**, *past* **dared**) to be brave enough to: *David* **dared** (**to**) *climb the tree. She* **daren't** (= dare not) *tell her sister that she has lost her money.*

dark¹ /dɑːk/ *adjective* **1** like night; not light or bright: *It was getting* **dark***, so we hurried home.* **2** of a deep colour, nearer black than white: *He wore a* **dark** *suit.* **darkness** *noun* (*no plural*): *We couldn't see the houses in the* **darkness***.*

dark² *noun* (*no plural*) the lack of light: *We could not see in the* **dark***.*

deadly /'dedlɪ/ *adjective* (**deadlier, deadliest**) causing death: *This seed is* **deadly** *if you eat it.*

deep /diːp/ *adjective* **1** going down a long way: *This is a* **deep** *river; it is 50 metres* **deep***. He has a* **deep** *voice.* **2** strong or dark in colour: *He has* **deep** *brown*

MINI-DICTIONARY

eyes. **3** felt strongly: *Her love for the child was very* **deep**. **depth** /depθ/ *noun*: *What is the* **depth** *of the river? Nobody knew the* **depth** *of her love for the child.*

deer /dɪəʳ/ *noun* (*plural* **deer**) an animal which has horns and which runs fast

defeat /dɪˈfiːt/ *verb* to beat; win over: *They were* **defeated** *in the football match.*

delay[1] /dɪˈleɪ/ *noun* a time of waiting: *There was a* **delay** *while Father went back to the house to get his money.*

delay[2] *verb* to make something take a longer time; wait: *The letter was* **delayed** *three days by the train accident.*

delicate /ˈdelɪkət/ *adjective* fine; easily harmed or broken: *a* **delicate** *glass/a* **delicate** *child who is often ill* **delicately** *adverb*: *He cleaned his mouth* **delicately** *with his handkerchief.*

delicious /dɪˈlɪʃəs/ *adjective* good to eat: *The soup is* **delicious**.

department store /dɪˈpɑːtmənt stɔː/ *noun* a big shop which sells most things

depend /dɪˈpend/ *verb* **1** to be a result of: *"Are you going for a walk?" "That* **depends on** *the weather." "Are you coming with us?" "It* **depends** (= I have some doubts about it)." **2** to need; trust: *She* **depends on** *him to take her to school every day. Can I* **depend on** *your help?*

desert /ˈdezət/ *noun* a large empty, usually very dry, place where almost nothing grows: *the Sahara* **desert**

desperate /ˈdesprət/ *adjective* ready to do anything to get what you want: *The man lost in the desert was* **desperate** *for water.*

destroy /dɪˈstrɔɪ/ *verb* to break up or get rid of completely: *The fire* **destroyed** *all my books.*

development /dɪˈveləpmənt/ *noun* **1** something new in the growth of something: *an exciting* **development** *in the story of the robbery* **2** (*no plural*) growing: *The* **development** *of this industry will take several years.*

disappear /ˌdɪsəˈpɪəʳ/ *verb* to go away; be no longer seen: *The boy* **disappeared** *round the corner.*

disappoint /ˌdɪsəˈpɔɪnt/ *verb* to be less interesting, nice, etc. than you expected, and so make you sad: *Don't be* **disappointed** *if you lose, next time you might win!* **disappointment** *noun*: *He could not hide his* **disappointment** *when his team lost the game.*

disaster /dɪˈzɑːstəʳ/ *noun* something very bad, especially something that happens to a lot of people: *The floods were a* **disaster**, *hundreds of people were killed and crops destroyed.*

disastrous /dɪˈzɑːstrəs/ *adjective* very bad or ending in failure: *We had a* **disastrous** *meeting last week – nobody agreed about anything.* **disastrously** *adverb*

disguise /dɪsˈgaɪz/ *noun* something that you wear to make you look like someone else

doll /dɒl/ *noun* a toy made to look like a person

dominate /ˈdɒmɪneɪt/ *verb* (*present participle* **dominating**, *past* **dominated**) to have power over: *That child* **dominates** *all the smaller children.*

double decker /ˈdʌbəl dekəʳ/ *noun* a bus with two floors

dream[1] /driːm/ *verb* (*present participle* **dreaming**, *past* **dreamt** /dremt/ *or* **dreamed** /driːmd/) **1** to imagine things while you are asleep: *I* **dreamt about** *my teacher last night.* **2** to imagine something nice: *I* **dream of** *being the best footballer in the town.*

dream[2] *noun* **1** something that you imagine while you are asleep: *a frightening* **dream** **2** something nice that you imagine, or that you want to do: *It is my* **dream** *to come first in the race.*

dynamic /daɪˈnæmɪk/ *adjective* full of new and exciting ideas and very active: *Our new head teacher is very* **dynamic** *– she wants to change everything.*

E

ecology /ɪˈkɒlədʒɪ/ *noun* (*no plural*) the study of the way plants, animals and people relate to each other and to their surroundings

edge /edʒ/ *noun* the outside end of something: *The* **edge** *of the plate was blue.*

elbow /ˈelbəʊ/ *noun* the part of your arm which bends it in the middle

elegant /ˈelɪgənt/ *adjective* graceful and beautiful: **elegant** *clothes*

emotion /ɪˈməʊʃn/ *noun* a feeling: *Anger and love are strong* **emotions**. **emotional** /ɪˈməʊʃənəl/ *adjective* having or causing strong feelings, especially sad ones: *I felt very* **emotional** *when we said goodbye. The novel was very* **emotional**. **emotionally** *adverb*

emperor /ˈemprəʳ/ *noun* a ruler of a country or several countries

empire /ˈempaɪəʳ/ *noun* a group of countries ruled by an emperor or empress

energy /ˈenədʒɪ/ *noun* (*no plural*) power to do things or to make things work: *I have no* **energy** *left after playing football. Coal and oil give us* **energy** *for heating, lighting, moving things, etc.* **energetic** /ˌenəˈdʒetɪk/ *adjective*: *He is an* **energetic** *boy; he enjoys sports.* **energetically** *adverb*

engineer /ˌendʒɪˈnɪəʳ/ *noun* a person who plans and makes machines, roads, bridges, etc. **engineering** *noun* (*no plural*) the science or job of an engineer: *He is studying* **engineering** *at college.*

enormous /ɪˈnɔːməs/ *adjective* very large: *an* **enormous** *plate of food*

enthusiasm /ɪnˈθjuːzɪæzm/ *noun* (*no plural*) an eager feeling of wanting to do something: *He plays football with* **enthusiasm**. **enthusiastic** /ɪnˌθjuːzɪˈæstɪk/ *adjective*: *She's very* **enthusiastic** *about her new job. an* **enthusiastic** *footballer* **enthusiastically** *adverb*: *"I'd love to come," she said* **enthusiastically**.

equipment /ɪˈkwɪpmənt/ *noun* (*no plural*) an item that is useful for doing something: *Our school has been given some new* **equipment** *– a radio and a television.*

escape /ɪˈskeɪp/ *verb* (*present participle* **escaping**, *past* **escaped**) to get free from: *to* **escape** *from prison*

everyday /ˌevrɪˈdeɪ/ *adjective* usual; not special: *This is an* **everyday** *dress; I shall wear something better to the party.*

exciting /ɪkˈsaɪtɪŋ/ *adjective* giving strong and pleasant feelings; causing to lose calmness: *an* **exciting** *film; What* **exciting** *news!*

excuse[1] /ɪkˈskjuːz/ *verb* (*present participle* **excusing**, *past* **excused**) to forgive: *I* **excused** *James's past bad work, as I knew he had been ill.* **Excuse me**, *could you tell me the way to the station?*

excuse[2] /ɪkˈskjuːs/ *noun* a reason given when you ask someone to forgive you: *I haven't done the work well; my* **excuse** *is that I have been ill.*

execute /ˈeksɪkjuːt/ *verb* (*present participle* **executing**, *past* **executed**) to kill as a punishment decided by law **exeˈcution** *noun*

exercise /ˈeksəsaɪz/ *noun* **1** using your body to make it stronger or more healthy: *Running is good* **exercise**. *We did some difficult* **exercises**. **2** a piece of work given in school: *I wrote in my* **exercise book**.

exhaust[1] /ɪgˈzɔːst/ *verb* to make very tired: *We are all* **exhausted** *after the journey. It was an* **exhausting** *day.*

exhaust[2] *noun* (*no plural*) burnt gas which comes out from the back of a car

expert /ˈekspɜːt/ *noun* a person who is very good at something special: *an* **expert** *in cookery/a cookery* **expert**

extinct /ɪkˈstɪŋkt/ *adjective* (of a plant or animal) no longer existing: *The elephant is becoming* **extinct**.

extreme /ɪkˈstriːm/ *adjective* the furthest possible: *She lives at the* **extreme** *edge of the forest.* **extremely** *adverb* very: *I am* **extremely** *hot.*

eyebrow /ˈaɪbraʊ/ *noun* the hairy line above the human eye

F

facilities /fəˈsɪlətɪz/ *plural noun* something for you to use, especially in a public place: *Are there washing* **facilities** *in the school?* (= is there somewhere you can wash, with soap, running water etc.?)

fact /fækt/ *noun* something that is true; something that has happened: *It is a* **fact** *that you are reading this sentence. I said it was Tuesday, but* **in fact** (= really) *it was Monday.*

factory /ˈfæktrɪ/ *noun* (*plural* **factories**) a place where things are made, often by machines

fang /fæŋ/ *noun* a long sharp tooth: *The dog growled and showed its* **fangs**.

fascinate /ˈfæsɪneɪt/ *verb* (*present participle* **fascinating**, *past* **fascinated**) to make someone feel very strong interest: *The city* **fascinates** *him. The programme was* **fascinating**.

fault /fɔːlt/ *noun* something that is wrong; a mistake or weak point: *His greatest*

115

fault is that he talks too much. Who broke the cup? It's my **fault**, I dropped it. **faultless** adjective having no faults; perfect: **faultless** work

feature /ˈfiːtʃəʳ/ noun 1 any part of the face, especially eyes, nose, and mouth: Her eyes were her best **feature**. 2 a part of something that you notice specially: The unusual fireplace was a **feature** of the room.

festival /ˈfestɪvl/ noun a time when people get together to amuse themselves, dance, sing, etc.

fiction /ˈfɪkʃən/ noun stories about imaginary people and events: Novels and short stories are works of **fiction**. Do you prefer **fiction** or non-fiction?

fierce /fɪəs/ adjective wild; angry; cruel: a **fierce** dog/a **fierce** storm **fiercely** adverb

fight /faɪt/ (present participle **fighting**, past **fought** /fɔːt/) to use your body or weapons against someone or something: What are the boys **fighting** about?

finger /ˈfɪŋgəʳ/ noun one of the five long parts of your hand

fit /fɪt/ verb (present participle **fitting**, past **fitted**) 1 to be the right size for: The trousers don't **fit** him, they are too small. 2 to fix something in place: He **fitted** a telephone in my office.

flight /flaɪt/ noun flying: The (aeroplane) **flight** took three hours. They saw the birds **in flight**.

flower /ˈflaʊəʳ/ noun the part of a plant which holds the seeds and which is usually brightly coloured

forename /ˈfɔːneɪm/ noun the name that your parents give you that stands before your surname (= family name): My name is Sarah Jane Brown; my **forenames** are Sarah and Jane.

found /faʊnd/ verb to start: He **founded** the school in 1954.

free /friː/ adjective not costing any money: Entrance to the museum is **free**.

frighten /ˈfraɪtn/ verb to make someone afraid: He was **frightened** of the fierce dog.

G

gas /gæs/ noun 1 any substance like air; not liquid or solid: The air we breathe is made chiefly of two **gases**. 2 (no plural) a gas got by burning coal and used to give heat: a **gas** cooker

general /ˈdʒenrəl/ noun an important officer in an army

generation /ˌdʒenəˈreɪʃn/ noun the people born at a certain time: My parents and I belong to different **generations**.

get /get/ verb (present participle **getting**, past **got** /gɒt/) 1 to have, have, or buy: I **got** a letter from Maria this morning. I must **get** some fruit in the market. I have **got** a dog. 2 to become: I **got** angry with him. 3 to make be or happen: He **got** the shirt clean in hot water. 4 to arrive: When we **got** to the station, the train was waiting. 5 must: I **have got to** see him today.

get around verb to move or travel from place to place: He doesn't **get around** much since his accident. They **get around** a lot – I see them everywhere I go.

get up verb to get out of bed: They're still in bed, they don't **get up** until 10 on Sundays.

ghost /gəʊst/ noun the form of a dead person which a living person thinks he/she sees '**ghostly** adjective frightening, as if there were ghosts

giant¹ /ˈdʒaɪənt/ noun a very large person, usually only talked about in stories

giant² adjective very large: a **giant** snake

give up /gɪv ˈʌp/ verb to stop: I've **given up** smoking. I can't guess the answer, I **give up** (= I have stopped trying to guess).

glare /gleəʳ/ verb (present participle **glaring**, past **glared**) 1 to shine with an unpleasantly bright light: The sun **glared** down. 2 to look hard and unpleasantly: She **glared** at me.

gloom /gluːm/ noun 1 darkness: In the **gloom** of the thick forest, he nearly lost his way. 2 a feeling of sadness: He was deep in **gloom** because his girlfriend had gone away. '**gloomy** adjective (**gloomier**, **gloomiest**) a **gloomy** day/a **gloomy** expression on his face

go /gəʊ/ verb (present participle **going** /ˈgəʊɪŋ/, past tense **went** /went/, past participle **gone** /gɒn/) to move: Are you **going** to school today? The food **goes** (= has a special place) in the cupboard. They **went out** to a party. When a light or a fire **goes out**, it stops shining or burning. I am **going to** wear (= will wear) the blue dress tomorrow. Will you **go through** this work (= look at it) and make sure there are no mistakes?

go down verb 1 to move towards a lower position: They **went down** the hill. 2 to become less: The number of students at our school has **gone down**.

go on verb 1 to happen: What's **going on**? 2 to continue: He **went on** talking as if nothing had happened.

gondola /ˈgɒndələ/ noun a long narrow boat used on the canals in Venice in Italy

graceful /ˈgreɪsfʊl/ adjective attractive in movement: that athlete runs **gracefully**.

gradual /ˈgrædʒʊəl/ adjective happening slowly: a **gradual** improvement in his work **gradually** /ˈgrædʒəli/ adverb slowly and in stages: The water **gradually** rose to the top of the pool.

grain /greɪn/ noun a seed or small piece of something: a few **grains** of salt

grape /greɪp/ noun a small round juicy fruit

gravity /ˈgrævəti/ noun (no plural) the force which brings things down to Earth: When you let go of something, **gravity** makes it fall to the floor.

green /griːn/ adjective 1 the colour of leaves and grass 2 about the protection of the natural world: I'm very interested in **green** issues. the **Green** party

greenhouse effect /griːnhaʊs ɪfekt/ noun the problem of the gradual warming of the air around the Earth

ground /graʊnd/ noun (no plural) the surface of the Earth: Trees grow in the **ground**. The **ground 'floor** of a building is on the same level as the ground. **grounds** plural noun garden or land around a building

grow /grəʊ/ verb (present participle **growing**, past **grew** /gruː/, past participle **grown** /grəʊn/) 1 to get bigger: Children **grow** (**up**) fast. I am **growing** an orange-tree (= I have planted the seed and I am waiting for it to get bigger). 2 to become: The weather **grew** colder.

grow up verb to become adult: I want to be a doctor when I **grow up**. She **grew up** (= spent her childhood) in Paris.

guess¹ /ges/ verb to give an answer that you feel may be right: I don't know how old David is – I **guess** he's five.

guess² noun something that you think is right, but do not know: If you don't know the answer, make a **guess**.

gymnasium /dʒɪmˈneɪzɪəm/ or **gym** /dʒɪm/ a hall where you carry out physical exercises

gymnastics /dʒɪmˈnæstɪks/ plural noun exercises for the body: We do **gymnastics** in a **gymnasium** /dʒɪmˈneɪzɪəm/.

H

habitat /ˈhæbɪtæt/ noun the place where a plant or animal naturally lives: Many animals have been forced to leave their natural **habitat**.

Halloween /ˌhæləʊˈiːn/ noun the night of October 31st, when witches and ghosts are supposed to appear

handwriting /ˈhændraɪtɪŋ/ noun writing done by hand, or the way a person writes: She has beautiful **handwriting**.

hang gliding /ˈhæŋ glaɪdɪŋ/ noun (no plural) a sport in which you fly through the air hanging from a hang glider (= an apparatus made of a large piece of cloth over a frame)

haunt /hɔːnt/ verb (of ghosts or spirits) to visit or be in a place: People say that old house is **haunted**.

health /helθ/ noun (no plural) the state of your body; how you are: His **health** is not good (= he is often ill). '**healthy** adjective (**healthier**, **healthiest**): You look very **healthy** (= well in body). It is **healthy** (= good for the health) to eat fruit.

height /haɪt/ noun how tall or far from the ground something is: He measured the **height** of the bridge.

helicopter /ˈhelɪkɒptəʳ/ noun a sort of aeroplane with blades which go round on its top, which can go straight up from the ground and stay still in the air

hesitate /ˈhezɪteɪt/ verb (present participle **hesitating**, past **hesitated**) to stop what you are doing for a short time: He **hesitated** before he answered because he didn't know what to say.

hibernate /ˈhaɪbəneɪt/ verb (of animals) to go into a state like a deep sleep in the

winter: *Bears* **hibernate** *in winter.*
history /ˈhɪstri/ *noun* (*no plural*) learning about the past: *a* **history** *lesson at school*
historic /hɪˈstɒrɪk/ *adjective* causing important changes: *a* **historic** *meeting between the two leaders* **historical** /hɪˈstɒrɪkl/ *adjective* of history; in or about the past: *a* **historical** *play*
hit /hɪt/ *noun* **1** a blow or stroke, especially a good one: *He aimed at the mark on the wall and hit it exactly – it was a good* **hit**. **2** something, such as a song or film, which is successful because many people like it: *That song was a* **hit** *last year.*
hockey /ˈhɒki/ *noun* (*no plural*) a game played by two teams who use curved sticks to hit a ball into a net
hope¹ /həʊp/ *verb* to wish for and expect: *I* **hope** *to go to college.*
hope² *noun* wishing and expecting: *I gave up* **hope** *of going to college when I failed my examinations.*
horoscope /ˈhɒrəskəʊp/ *noun* a description of someone's character and future life based on the position of the stars and planets when they were born
horrible /ˈhɒrəbl/ *adjective* very unpleasant: *There was a* **horrible** *accident here yesterday.* **horribly** *adverb*
horrify /ˈhɒrɪfaɪ/ *verb* (*present participle* **horrifying**, *past* **horrified**) to shock or make someone feel fear: *I was* **horrified** *by the news.*
horror /ˈhɒrəʳ/ *noun* great fear and shock: *The man saw with* **horror** *that there had been a bad accident.*
hover /ˈhɒvəʳ/ *verb* to stay in the air without moving: *Some birds* **hover** *when they look for animals to kill on the ground.*
howl /haʊl/ *verb* to cry loudly and with a long breath: *The dog* **howled** *when it was shut in the house. Wind* **howled** *round the house.* **howl** *noun*
hummingbird /ˈhʌmɪŋbɜːd/ *noun* a small brightly coloured bird which moves its wings so quickly that they make a musical noise
hurt /hɜːt/ *verb* (*past* **hurt**) to give pain or cause damage: *My leg* **hurts**. *I* **hurt** *it playing football. She's* **hurt** (= sad) *because you haven't visited her.*
hypnotise /ˈhɪpnətaɪz/ *verb* to put someone into a state in which they seem to be asleep but can respond to questions and instructions: *She* **hypnotised** *him into stopping smoking.*

I

impressive /ɪmˈpresɪv/ *adjective* causing strong good feelings or thought: *The building is very* **impressive**. *Her work is* **impressive**.
improve /ɪmˈpruːv/ (*present participle* **improving**, *past* **improved**) to make or get better: *Your reading has* **improved** *this year, but you must try to* **improve** *your writing.*
improvise /ˈɪmprəvaɪz/ *verb* to do or make something without planning or following normal procedure: *I'd lost my notes so I had to* **improvise** *my speech. We* **improvised** *a meal with potatoes and onions.*
industry /ˈɪndəstri/ *noun* (*plural* **industries**) making things in factories: *Our town has a lot of* **industry**. *What are the important* **industries** *in the town?*
initiative /ɪˈnɪʃətɪv/ *noun* (*no plural*) the ability to decide and to act without asking other people to help: *They showed a lot of* **initiative** *in organising the class play by themselves.*
injure /ˈɪndʒəʳ/ *verb* (*present participle* **injuring**, *past* **injured**) to harm; wound: *There were two people* **injured** *in the car accident.* **injury** *noun* (*plural* **injuries**) a wound; damage: *The people in the accident had serious* **injuries**.
island /ˈaɪlənd/ *noun* a piece of land surrounded by water
issue /ˈɪʃuː/ *noun* an important subject to talk about: *Ecology is one of the main* **issues** *to be discussed at the meeting.*

J

jog /dʒɒg/ *verb* (*present participle* **jogging**, *past* **jogged**) to run slowly as a form of exercise: *She goes* **jogging** *every morning.*
joke¹ /dʒəʊk/ *noun* something you say or do to make people laugh: *Our teacher told us a* **joke** *today. We all* **played a joke on** *him* (= did something to make other people laugh at him).
joke² *verb* (*present participle* **joking**, *past* **joked**) to tell jokes: *I didn't mean that seriously – I was only* **joking**.
journey /ˈdʒɜːni/ *noun* a trip, usually a long one: *How long is the* **journey** *to the coast?*
judo /ˈdʒuːdəʊ/ *noun* (*no plural*) a kind of fighting in which you hold and throw the other person
jump¹ /dʒʌmp/ *verb* **1** to move the body off the ground, up in the air, or over something: *She* **jumped up** *into the chair. The dog* **jumped over** *the gate.* **2** to move quickly: *She* **jumped to her feet** (=stood up quickly). **3** to move suddenly because of fear or surprise: *That sudden noise made me* **jump**.
jump² *noun* **1** moving the body off the ground: *He went over the fence in one* **jump**. **2** something that someone jumps over, in a race, etc.: *The horses raced over the* **jumps**.

K

karate /kəˈrɑːti/ *noun* (*no plural*) a kind of fighting in which you hit and kick the other person
keep /kiːp/ *verb* (*past* **kept** /kept/) **1** to have or hold something: *I don't want this book any more, so you can* **keep** *it* (= have it as your own). *Can I* **keep** *this book until next week, and give it back to you then?* **2** to store something in a place: *Always* **keep** *your money in a safe place.* **3** to give food, clothes, and things that are needed to someone: *They have to earn quite a lot of money to* **keep** *their six children.* **4** to stay or make someone stay: *Her illness* **kept** *her in hospital for three weeks.* **Keep** *still while I'm cutting your hair. She* **keeps** *telling me* (= she tells me often) *but I always forget. Danger –* **keep out**! **Keep off** *the grass!*
kick /kɪk/ *verb* to hit something with the foot; move the foot suddenly as if to hit something: *Don't* **kick** *the ball into the road. The baby was lying on its back,* **kicking** *its legs in the air.*
kidnap /ˈkɪdnæp/ *verb* (*present participle* **kidnapping**, *past* **kidnapped**) to take someone away and ask for money in return for bringing them back safely **kidnapper** *noun*
kill /kɪl/ *verb* to make someone or something die: *Ten people were* **killed** *in the train crash.*
kit /kɪt/ *noun* (*no plural*) all the things needed for doing something or going somewhere: *She put her basketball* **kit** *into the bag.*
knee /niː/ *noun* the joint in the middle of the leg where the leg bends

L

label /ˈleɪbl/ *noun* a piece of paper or other material fixed to something which gives you information about it: *A* **label** *on a parcel tells us where to send it.*
land /lænd/ *verb* **1** to come to the ground or the land from the air or water: *The plane will* **land** *in five minutes.* **2** to bring a plane or ship to the ground from the air or water: *He* **landed** *the plane at the airport.* **landing** *noun: The plane made a safe* **landing**.
lane /leɪn/ *noun* a narrow road: *We walked down the* **lane** *to the farm.*
launch /lɔːntʃ/ *verb* to put a ship into the water or to send a spaceship into space
layer /ˈleɪəʳ/ *noun* a covering that is spread on top of another thing or in between two other things: *This cake has a* **layer** *of chocolate in the middle.*
lean /liːn/ *verb* (*past* **leaned** *or* **leant** /lent/) to bend forwards, sideways, backwards, or towards: *Do not* **lean** *out of the window too far because you might fall out.*
length /leŋθ/ *noun* (*no plural*) the distance from one end of something to the other; how long something is: *Mary's dress is not the right* **length**; *it is too short.*
liberate /ˈlɪbəreɪt/ *verb* (*present participle* **liberating**, *past* **liberated**) to make someone free: *The prisoners were* **liberated** *from the camp in 1945.*
lie /laɪ/ *verb* (*present participle* **lying**, *past tense* **lay** /leɪ/, *past participle* **lain** /leɪn/) to have your body flat on something: *He was* **lying** *in the shade of the tree. She* **lay**

MINI-DICTIONARY

down (= got into a lying position) *on her bed.*
lightbulb /'laɪtbʌlb/ *noun* a round glass object with a wire inside which gives out light: *She put a new **lightbulb** in the lamp.*
line /laɪn/ *verb (present participle **lining**, past **lined**)* to stand in a line: *People **lined** the streets to see the famous man go past.* **Line up** please, children!
lock /lɒk/ *verb* to close a door with a key: *My father accidentally **locked** me **out** of the house* (= he locked the door so that I could not get back into the house).
locker /'lɒkə^r/ *noun* a small cupboard, often with a lock, for keeping things: *At the station there were **lockers** where people could leave suitcases.*
log book /'lɒg bʊk/ *noun* a ship's diary
logical /'lɒdʒɪkəl/ *adjective* having good sense; thinking clearly and carefully: *It seemed the **logical** thing to do. She has a **logical** mind.*
look /lʊk/ *verb* **1** to point the eyes towards a thing to try to see it: *The teacher told us to **look** at the blackboard.* **Look out** (= be careful), *there's a car coming. The children were **looking for** (= trying to find) a ball. My friend **looked after** (= cared for) my dog while I was on holiday. When you do not understand a word, you can **look it up** (= find it) in this dictionary. We are all **looking forward** to our holiday* (= waiting for it and thinking about it with pleasure). **2** to seem to be: *That dog **looks** dangerous. That **looks like** an interesting film.*
lost /lɒst/ *adjective* not knowing where you are: *The little boy went for a walk and got **lost**.*
lovely /'lʌvlɪ/ *adjective* (**lovelier, loveliest**) very much liked; very beautiful: *a **lovely** cool drink/a **lovely** dress*
luck /lʌk/ *noun* (no plural) the good and bad things that happen to you by chance: *It was good **luck** that I met you here; I did not expect to see you.*

M

magical /'mædʒɪkəl/ *adjective* of strange power, mystery or beauty: *a **magical** evening*
magnificent /mæg'nɪfɪsnt/ *adjective* very great; very fine: *What a **magnificent** building!*
manufacture /ˌmænjʊ'fæktʃə^r/ *verb (present participle **manufacturing**, past **manufactured**)* to make things in large numbers, usually by machinery: *to **manufacture** goods in a factory*
marsh /mɑːʃ/ *noun* (plural **marshes**) low, wet ground: *When they tried to cross the **marsh**, their shoes sank into the soft ground.*
mask /mɑːsk/ *noun* a covering to hide the face: *We all wore **masks** at the party and no one knew who we were.*
match /mætʃ/ *noun* (plural **matches**) a game between two people or two teams: *a football **match***

material /mə'tɪərɪəl/ *adjective* solid and physical, not spiritual: *Food is a **material** need.*
medal /'medl/ *noun* a piece of metal like a coin given to someone who has done something special
message /'mesɪdʒ/ *noun* news or an order sent from one person to another: *I have sent mother a **message** to tell her I shall be home late.*
migrate /maɪ'greɪt/ *verb (present participle **migrating**, past **migrated**)* to travel at the same time every year from one part of the world to another: *Some birds **migrate** to find warmer weather.*
mill /mɪl/ *noun* a place where things are made by machinery: *Cotton is made in a cotton **mill**.*
mine[1] /maɪn/ *noun* a deep hole in the ground from which people take out coal, iron, gold, etc.
mine[2] *verb (present participle **mining**, past **mined**)* to dig out something from a mine: *They **were mining** for silver.*
mineral /'mɪnrəl/ *noun* a substance like iron, coal, or oil which is taken out of the ground
miss /mɪs/ *verb* not to hit or catch something: *He threw the ball to me, but I **missed** it and it landed on the ground. I was late because I **missed** the bus.*
mist /mɪst/ *noun* a thin cloud near the ground: *We couldn't see through the **mist**.*
misty *adjective* (**mistier, mistiest**): **misty** weather
mix /mɪks/ *verb* to put different things together to make something new; join together: *We **mix** flour and water to make bread.* **mixture** /'mɪkstʃə^r/ *noun:* *A **mixture** is what we make by putting different things together.*
monastery /'mɒnəstrɪ/ *noun* (plural **monasteries**) a place where monks live
monk /mʌŋk/ *noun* one of a group of men who live together and have given their lives to a religion
monorail /'mɒnəreɪl/ *noun* a railway system with only one rail, or a train that travels along such a system
monster /'mɒnstə^r/ *noun* an animal or person with a strange or unusual shape, often very big
monumental /ˌmɒnjə'mentl/ *adjective* very big and important: *The cathedral is of **monumental** proportions.*
murder[1] /'mɜːdə^r/ *verb* to kill a person when you have decided to do it **murderer** *noun* a person who murders someone
murder[2] *noun* an act of murdering: *Murder is a serious crime.*
muscle /'mʌsl/ *noun* one of the pieces of stretchy material in the body which can tighten to move parts of the body: *We use our **muscles** to bend our arms and legs.*
mystery /'mɪstərɪ/ *noun* (plural **mysteries**) a strange thing which we cannot explain: *Who had taken the money? It was a **mystery**.* **mysterious** /mɪ'stɪərɪəs/ *adjective:* *a **mysterious** visitor*

N

narrow /'nærəʊ/ *adjective* not wide; small from side to side: *a **narrow** path*
narrowly /'nærəʊlɪ/ *adverb* only just: *We **narrowly** avoided an accident.*
neck /nek/ *noun* the part of the body between the head and shoulders
nectar /'nektə^r/ *noun* the sweet liquid which bees obtain from flowers
nest /nest/ *noun* the home built by a bird or by some animals and insects: *The bird laid three eggs in her **nest**.*
net /net/ *noun* material with open spaces between knotted thread, string, or wire: *The footballer kicked the ball into the back of the **net**. A fishing **net** is spread out under water to catch fish.*
neutral /'njuːtrəl/ *adjective* not having strong feelings or opinions for or against a subject: *The documentary tried to give a **neutral** picture of the problems.*
news /njuːz/ *plural noun (used with a singular verb)* things which have just happened: *We listen to the **news** on the radio.*
nightmare /'naɪtmeə^r/ *noun* a very bad dream: *He had **nightmares** about his exams.*
noble[1] /'nəʊbl/ *adjective* (**nobler, noblest**) of one of the old important families
noble[2] *noun* a member of a very old and important family
nobody /'nəʊbədɪ/ or **no one** /'nəʊ wʌn/ not anybody; no person: *I knocked on the door but **nobody** opened it.*
noise /nɔɪz/ *noun* a loud sound, often unpleasant: *Planes make a lot of **noise**. My car's making strange **noises**.* **'noisily** *adverb* **'noisy** *adjective* (**noisier, noisiest**): *"What a **noisy** class you are!" said the teacher.*
northwest /ˌnɔːθ'west/ *noun, adjective, adverb* between the north and the west
nothing /'nʌθɪŋ/ *noun* not any thing: *There is **nothing** in this box – it is empty. I got this bicycle for **nothing*** (= free).
notice[1] /'nəʊtɪs/ *noun* a warning; news in writing that something is going to happen or has happened: *The **notice** on the door said that the library was closed. There were lots of notices on the **notice-board*** (= a piece of wood on a wall on which you put a notice).
notice[2] *verb (present participle **noticing**, past **noticed**)* to see: *The prisoner **noticed** that the door was open and ran away.*
nuclear /'njuːklɪə^r/ *adjective* describing a kind of energy: **nuclear** *power*; **nuclear** *weapons*

O

office block /'ɒfɪs blɒk/ *noun* a big, usually tall building divided into offices
old-fashioned /ˌəʊld 'fæʃənd/ not modern; not common any more: ***old-fashioned** clothes*
opera /'ɒprə/ *noun* a kind of play which has songs and music instead of spoken words

118

optimistic /ˌɒptɪˈmɪstɪk/ *adjective* always hopeful about the future and thinking that only good things will happen: *I'm very **optimistic** about the tests – I'm sure we'll all pass.*

orbit /ˈɔːbɪt/ *verb* to move in an orbit round something: *The spaceship **orbited** the moon.*

orphan /ˈɔːfn/ *noun* someone whose mother and father are dead **orphanage** *noun* a home for orphan children

overboard /ˈəʊvəbɔːd/ *adverb* over the side of a boat into the water: *He fell **overboard**.*

ozone /ˈəʊzəʊn/ *noun* (*no plural*) a type of oxygen (= a gas) which forms a layer around the Earth: *The **ozone layer** is being damaged by pollution.*

P

pacifist /ˈpæsɪfɪst/ *noun* a person who believes that wars are wrong and will not fight in them

palace /ˈpæləs/ *noun* a large building where an important person, such as a king, lives

pale /peɪl/ *adjective* (**paler, palest**) light or white in colour: *The sky was **pale** blue. The baby had **pale** skin.*

parachute¹ /ˈpærəʃuːt/ *noun* a large round piece of cloth that fills with air, and lets someone fall slowly to earth from an aeroplane

parachute² *verb* to jump from an aeroplane and fall slowly to the ground with the help of a parachute: *They enjoy **parachuting** on Saturdays.*

part /pɑːt/ *noun* a character in a play or film: *James acted the **part** of the soldier in the play.*

passage /ˈpæsɪdʒ/ *noun* a narrow path or part of a building: *Sarah's mother was waiting in the **passage** outside the doctor's room.*

passion /ˈpæʃn/ *noun* a very strong feeling, especially of love or anger: *She spoke with **passion** about human rights.* **passionate** *adjective* with very strong feelings: *She made a **passionate** speech.*

P.E. /ˌpiː ˈiː/ *noun* (*no plural*) short for physical education; games and exercises for the body: *P.E. is my favourite lesson at school.*

peaceful /ˈpiːsfəl/ *adjective* quiet: *It's **peaceful** at home when the children are at school.* **peacefully** *adverb*

peacock /ˈpiːkɒk/ *noun* a bird with a large brightly coloured tail

penfriend /ˈpenfrend/ *noun* a person, often in another country, whom you may not have met, but to whom you write letters: *Jane's got a **penfriend** in Russia.*

pessimistic /ˌpesɪˈmɪstɪk/ *adjective* never hopeful about the future and thinking that only bad things will happen: *He was feeling very **pessimistic** about the exams – he was sure he would fail.*

pink /pɪŋk/ *noun, adjective* (of) the colour made by mixing red and white

planet /ˈplænɪt/ *noun* one of the large masses like the Earth that go round a sun

plastic /ˈplæstɪk/ *adjective* a strong manmade substance used for strong containers, toys, etc.: *If you drop a **plastic** bowl, it will not break.*

play /pleɪ/ *verb* 1 to amuse yourself; take part in a game: *The children were **playing** with a ball. He **plays** football.* 2 to make sounds on a musical instrument: *She **plays** the drum.* 3 to act a part in a play or film: *She **played** the part of Juliet.*

pointed /ˈpɔɪntɪd/ *adjective* sharp at one end: *a **pointed** stick*

poison /ˈpɔɪzn/ *noun* (*no plural*) a substance which kills or harms you if it gets into your body **poisonous** *adjective*: *a **poisonous** snake*

pollute /pəˈluːt/ *verb* (*present participle* **polluting**, *past* **polluted**) to make the air, water, earth, etc., dirty and dangerous for people, animals and plants: *Nearby factories are **polluting** the air and water of the town.* **pollution** *noun* (*no plural*): ***Pollution** of the air, water and earth is destroying our planet.*

poorhouse /ˈpʊəhaʊs/ *noun* in the past, in Britain, a place where very poor people could live

popular /ˈpɒpjʊləʳ/ *adjective* liked by many people: *She is **popular** at school. This dance is **popular** with young people.*

port /pɔːt/ *noun* a place where boats are safe

power /ˈpaʊəʳ/ (*no plural*) 1 strength or force: *Electricity is a type of **power**.* 2 control over people and places: *The President has a lot of **power**.* **powerful** *adjective*: *The President is **powerful**.* **powerfully** *adverb*

power station /ˈpaʊəʳ ˌsteɪʃən/ *noun* a place where electricity is produced

practical /ˈpræktɪkl/ *adjective* about or good at doing rather than thinking: *He is very **practical** – he can make or mend almost anything.*

pretty *adverb* fairly; quite: *It was a **pretty** serious accident.*

programme /ˈprəʊɡræm/ *noun* 1 a list of things which are planned to happen: *A **programme** for a play contains a list of the actors' names and other information about the play.* 2 something sent out by radio or television: *We watched a **programme** about farming.*

prosperity /prɒˈsperətɪ/ *noun* (*no plural*) richness; having a lot of money or success or good luck **prosperous** /ˈprɒspərəs/ *adjective* rich: *a **prosperous** family*

psychic /ˈsaɪkɪk/ *adjective* able to use the mind in unusual ways, for example, to see into the future

pull /pʊl/ *verb* to move something towards yourself or by going in front of it: *He **pulled** his hand out of the hot water. A horse **pulled** the cart along the road. The house is going to be **pulled down**, as it is not safe.*

R

race¹ /reɪs/ *noun* a competition to see who can run, swim, walk, etc., fastest: *Jane can run fast – she usually wins **races**.*

race² *verb* (*present participle* **racing**, *past* **raced**) to try to run or go faster than: *Paul **raced** (**against**) John in the one mile race.*

rainbow /ˈreɪnbəʊ/ *noun* an arch of colours in the sky, especially after rain

rainforest /ˈreɪnfɒrɪst/ *noun* a forest in areas where there is a lot of rain: *The tropical **rainforests** are being destroyed.*

raise /reɪz/ *verb* (*present participle* **raising**, *past* **raised**) to lift up; make higher: *He **raised** his arms above his head. Her wages were **raised** last week.*

range /reɪndʒ/ *noun* 1 a line of mountains or hills 2 a number of different things: *We sell a wide **range** of goods.* 3 the distance something can reach or travel: *What is the **range** of your gun (= how far can you fire it)?*

rare /reəʳ/ *adjective* (**rarer, rarest**) not happening often; not often seen: *That bird is very **rare** in this country.*

rational /ˈræʃənl/ *adjective* having or showing good sense; able to think clearly and with reason: *Let's try to be **rational**. a **rational** argument/explanation*

raw /rɔː/ *adjective* 1 not cooked: ***raw** meat* 2 in the natural state; not changed: *Clay and water are the **raw** materials used for making pots.*

realise /ˈrɪəlaɪz/ *verb* (*present participle* **realising**, *past* **realised**) to know or understand something as true, especially suddenly: *When I heard the noise on the roof, I **realised** that it was raining.*

reason /ˈriːzn/ *noun* 1 why something is done or happens: *The **reason** she was ill was that she had eaten bad meat.* 2 (*no plural*) the power of thinking and deciding: *Use your **reason** – you can't expect to pass the examination if you don't work!*

reasonable *adjective* 1 having good sense: *Don't be afraid to talk to the teacher, she's very **reasonable**.* 2 fair: *a **reasonable** price* **reasonably** *adverb*

record /ˈrekɔːd/ *noun* 1 a round thin flat piece of plastic that stores sounds, and which we play on a machine (a **record player**) to hear the sounds 2 information that is written down and kept: *The doctor keeps a **record** of all the serious illnesses in the village.* 3 something done better, quicker, etc. than anyone else has done it: *He holds the world **record** for the high jump. Can anyone **break his record** (= do better)?*

recover /rɪˈkʌvəʳ/ *verb* to get better, or get back to a usual state: *She has had a bad illness, but she is **recovering** now.*

recycle /ˌriːˈsaɪkl/ *verb* (*present participle* **recycling**, *past* **recycled**) to treat something so that it can be used again: *Glass bottles, aluminium cans, and newspapers and magazines can all be **recycled**.*

relax /rɪˈlæks/ *verb* to become less worried, angry, tight, etc.: *Don't worry about it, just try to **relax**. We had a **relaxing** day at the seaside.*

religious /rɪˈlɪdʒəs/ adjective believing in one or more gods: *Jane is very religious. We have religious education classes at school.*

repair /rɪˈpeə^r/ verb to make something that is broken or old good again; mend: *Have you repaired the bicycle yet?*

reserve /rɪˈzɜːv/ noun a place where wild animals and plants live and are protected: *Africa has many game reserves. a nature reserve*

retire /rɪˈtaɪə^r/ verb (present participle retiring, past retired) to stop work because of old age or illness: *He retired from the business when he was 65.*

right /raɪt/ noun 1 (no plural) what is fair and good: *You must learn the difference between right and wrong.* 2 what is or should be allowed by law: *We must work for equal rights for everyone.* 3 the side opposite to the left side: *The school is on the left of the road, and his house is on the right.*

rocket /ˈrɒkɪt/ noun a thing driven into the air by burning gas, used to lift a weapon or a spaceship from the ground

romance /rəʊˈmæns/ noun 1 being in love: *a romance between a king and a poor girl* 2 a story about love **romantic** adjective: *a romantic love story; We had a romantic evening.*

rubber¹ /ˈrʌbə^r/ noun 1 (no plural) a soft material from a tree that can be stretched and that goes back into shape when it is let go: *Tyres are made of rubber.* 2 a piece of this material used for getting rid of pencil marks

rubber² adjective made of rubber: **rubber boots**

rush hour /ˈrʌʃ aʊə^r/ noun the time of day when there is most traffic

S

sail /seɪl/ verb 1 to travel on water: *His ship sails today.* 2 to direct a boat with sails: *She sailed the boat without any help.* '**sailor** noun a person who works on a ship

sand /sænd/ noun (no plural) fine powder, usually white or yellow, made of rock, often found next to the sea and in deserts

save /seɪv/ verb (present participle saving, past saved) 1 to help someone or something to be safe: *I saved the animals from the flood.* 2 to keep something until it is wanted: *If you save (money) now, you will be able to buy a car soon.* 3 to use less: *We should save oil, or else there won't be any left in the world.*

scared /skeəd/ adjective afraid, frightened

science /ˈsaɪəns/ noun the study of nature and the way things in the world are made, behave, etc.: *The chief sciences are chemistry, physics, and biology.*

science-fiction /ˌsaɪəns ˈfɪkʃən/ noun (no plural) stories about the future or about life on other planets: *I love science-fiction films.*

score /skɔː^r/ verb (present participle scoring, past scored) to win: *to score a point*

scream /skriːm/ verb to give a loud high cry: *He screamed with fear.*

scruffy /ˈskrʌfi/ adjective (**scruffier, scruffiest**) untidy and dirty: *He was wearing a scruffy old jacket.*

season /ˈsiːzən/ noun one of the four parts of the year; a special time of year: *Summer is the hottest season.*

secret /ˈsiːkrɪt/ noun, adjective something that has not been told to other people: *Don't tell anyone about our plan, keep it a secret – it's a secret plan.*

servant /ˈsɜːvənt/ noun a person who works for someone in his or her house: *They have two servants; a cook and a gardener.*

set up /ˌset ˈʌp/ verb (present participle setting up, past set up) 1 to put in position: *We quickly set up the tables for the school party.* 2 to start something like a business or organisation: *She set up the business in 1990.*

sewage /ˈsjuːɪdʒ/ noun water and waste material from the human body carried in sewers: *The city needs a new sewage disposal system.*

sex /seks/ noun 1 being male or female: *Which sex is your cat?* 2 what is done between a male and a female to make babies

sex symbol /ˈseks sɪmbəl/ noun a famous, attractive person: *Marilyn Monroe was a famous Hollywood sex symbol.*

shallow /ˈʃæləʊ/ adjective not deep: *The sea is shallow here.*

shark /ʃɑːk/ noun a large dangerous fish with sharp teeth

sharp /ʃɑːp/ adjective able to see things far away or very small: **sharp** *eyes*

shine /ʃaɪn/ verb (present participle shining, past shone /ʃɒn/) to give out light, or to throw back light: *The sun shines. He works at a slow speed. The water shone in the sunlight.* '**shiny** adjective (**shinier, shiniest**): **shiny** *shoes*

ship /ʃɪp/ noun a large boat that goes on the sea

shocked /ʃɒkt/ adjective very surprised

shop verb (present participle shopping, past shopped) to buy things: *We often shop in King's Road. Let's go shopping this afternoon.*

shore /ʃɔː^r/ noun the flat land at the edge of the sea or a large area of water: *We walked along the seashore.*

shrew /ʃruː/ noun a small animal like a mouse with a long nose

silk /sɪlk/ noun (no plural) a fine cloth made from the threads that come from a silkworm

silkworm /ˈsɪlkwɜːm/ noun a small creature that makes silk

sinister /ˈsɪnɪstə^r/ adjective seeming to intend something very bad: *He was a sinister figure, dressed in black with dark glasses.*

size /saɪz/ noun how big something or someone is: *What size is your house? The two books were the same size. These shoes are size 5.*

skate /skeɪt/ verb (present participle skating, past skated) to move smoothly over ice or on wheels over the ground: *She skated over the ice towards us. He loves roller skating.*

skateboard /ˈskeɪtbɔːd/ noun a narrow board with small wheels on which you can ride for fun or sport

ski¹ /skiː/ noun a long, thin, narrow piece of wood, plastic or metal, used in pairs for travelling in snow and for sport

ski² verb (present participle **skiing**, past **skied**) to go on skis, especially for sport: *I love skiing. We went on a skiing holiday.*

skin /skɪn/ noun the outside of a person, animal, vegetable, or fruit: *You can make shoes from the skins of animals.*

slide /slaɪd/ verb (present participle sliding, past slid /slɪd/) to move smoothly over a surface: *She fell over and slid across the shiny floor.*

sloth /sləʊθ/ noun a South American animal which moves very slowly

smash /smæʃ/ verb to break into pieces: *She smashed a cup.*

snowball /ˈsnəʊbɔːl/ noun a ball made from snow, which children throw at each other

solar /ˈsəʊlə^r/ adjective of or using the sun: **solar** *heat*

somebody /ˈsʌmbədi/ or **someone** 1 any person: *If you don't know the answer, ask somebody.* 2 some unknown person, or a person the speaker does not name: *There is somebody knocking at the door. I know somebody who lives near you.*

spear /spɪə^r/ noun a long thin weapon with a pointed end

species /ˈspiːʃiːz/ noun (plural **species**) sort; type: *a species of animal*

spectacular /spekˈtækjələ^r/ adjective very impressive and exciting: *He made a spectacular jump from the roof.*

speed /spiːd/ noun how fast something moves: *The speed of the car was frightening. He works at a slow speed.*

spend /spend/ verb (present participle spending, past spent) 1 to give out money: *How much money do you spend each week?* 2 to pass or use time: *I spent an hour reading.*

spider /ˈspaɪdə^r/ noun a small creature with eight legs, which uses threads from its body to catch insects in a web

spin /spɪn/ verb (present participle spinning, past spun /spʌn/) to go round and round fast: *The wheels of the car were spinning (round).*

spot /spɒt/ noun a (small) mark: *There was a spot of blood on the carpet.*

squash /skwɒʃ/ noun (no plural) a game played indoors with rackets and a small ball

stadium /ˈsteɪdiəm/ noun an open place where games and races are held; it has seats round it

star¹ /stɑː^r/ noun 1 a small point of light that can be seen in the sky at night 2 a five-pointed shape (★) 3 a famous or very skilful actor/actress, sportsperson, singer, etc.: *a film star/a football star*

star² verb (present participle **starring**, past **starred**) to appear as the main actor/actress: *Madonna starred in the film.*

start /stɑːt/ verb to begin: *If you are ready, you may start your work. The children started singing. We started off*

120

MINI-DICTIONARY

(= began our journey) *for Paris at dawn.*

stick¹ /stɪk/ *noun* a long thin piece of wood: *We made the fire out of dry* **sticks.** *The old man walked leaning on a* **stick.**

stick² *verb* (*present participle* **sticking,** *past* **stuck** /stʌk/) **1** to fix with a special substance (**glue**): *I* **stuck** *a stamp on the letter.* **2** to stay fixed: *The wheels of the car* **stuck** *in the mud and we could not go on.*

stick out *verb* hold or put out: *Don't* **stick** *your head* **out** *of the train window.*

stomach /ˈstʌmək/ *noun* the part of the body into which the food goes when it is swallowed

straighten /ˈstreɪtn/ *verb* to make or become straight: *Sit up and* **straighten** *your back.*

strange /streɪndʒ/ *adjective* (**stranger, strangest**) **1** odd; unusual: *a* **strange** *sound* **2** not what you are used to: *a* **strange** *city* **'strangely** *adverb*: *He acted* **strangely** *when he was ill.* **'stranger** *noun* a person you do not know

stress /stres/ *noun* **1** (*no plural*) a state of difficulty: *The* **stress** *of working for examinations made him ill.* **2** (*plural* **stresses**) saying a word or a part of a word with special force: *In the word "chemistry" the* **stress** *is on the first part of the word.*

stretch /stretʃ/ *verb* **1** to make or become larger or longer by pulling; pull tightly: *She* **stretched** *the material. Rubber* **stretches. 2** to make as long as possible: *He* **stretched** *his legs in front of him.* **3** to try and reach: *I* **stretched out** *my hand towards the book.*

strict /strɪkt/ *adjective* severe, especially about behaviour: *Our teacher is* **strict;** *we have to do what she says.* **'strictly** *adverb*

stuck /stʌk/ *adjective* unable to move: *The fly was* **stuck** *in the honey.*

studious /ˈstjuːdɪəs/ *adjective* fond of studying: *He's a quiet,* **studious** *boy.* **studiously** *adverb*

success /səkˈses/ *noun* **1** (*no plural*) succeeding: *his* **success** *in the examination* **2** (*plural* **successes**) a thing which succeeds: *Her party was a* **success;** *everyone enjoyed it.* **successful** *adjective* **successfully** *adverb*

sundial /ˈsʌndaɪəl/ *noun* an apparatus, used especially in the past, which tells the time from the sun

superb /suːˈpɜːb/ *adjective* very fine: *Her dancing is* **superb.**

supper /ˈsʌpəʳ/ *noun* an evening meal: *What would you like for* **supper?**

supply¹ /səˈplaɪ/ *noun* (*plural* **supplies**) a store which can be used; an amount: *We keep a large* **supply** *of food in the house. Our* **supplies** (= the things we need) *for this month are in the cupboard.*

supply² *verb* (*present participle* **supplying,** *past* **supplied**) to give or sell what is needed: *That company* **supplies** *paper to the printers.*

survive /səˈvaɪv/ *verb* (*present participle* **surviving,** *past* **survived**) to go on living: *The man was very ill, but he* **survived.** **survivor** *noun*: *There were two* **survivors** *from the accident.*

suspended animation /səsˈpendɪd ænɪˈmeɪʃən/ *noun* (*no plural*) a temporary state in which the main body functions of an animal slow down, so that it seems dead

sweet /swiːt/ *adjective* **1** like sugar or ripe fruit to taste: *I don't like* **sweet** *coffee, I like it better without sugar in it.* **2** pleasant or loving: *What a* **sweet** *smile she has!* **sweetly** *adverb*: *He smiled* **sweetly** *at his mother.*

T

tackle /ˈtækl/ *verb* (*present participle* **tackling,** *past* **tackled**) to try to stop someone: *He* **tackled** *the other player and kicked the ball across the field.*

take /teɪk/ *verb* (*present participle* **taking,** *past* **took** /tʊk/, *past participle* **taken**) **1** to get hold of something: *The mother* **took** *her child by the hand.* **2** to carry something or go with someone to another place: **Take** *this shopping home. Who has* **taken** *my chocolate? Will you* **take** *me to town today?* **3** to swallow something: *I* **took** *the medicine.* **4** to travel in a vehicle: *to* **take** *a train* **5** to need: *I will* **take** *an hour to cook the dinner.* **6** (used in sentences like these): **Take down** (= write) *this sentence.* **Take off** (= remove) *your clothes: they're very wet. The plane* **took off** (= left the ground) *at three o'clock.*

take on /teɪk ɒn/ *verb* **1** to give a job to: *He was* **taken on** *as an office boy.* **2** to accept work, responsibility, a challenge, etc.: *She decided to* **take on** *the challenge of the new job.*

talent /ˈtælənt/ *noun* the ability to do something well: *My sister has a* **talent** *for singing.*

teacher's pet /ˈtiːtʃəz pet/ *noun* a teacher's favourite student

technology /tekˈnɒlədʒɪ/ *noun* (*no plural*) using the knowledge we get through science to make things in factories, build things, etc.: *the new* **technology** *of micro* (= very small) *computers*

telescope /ˈtelɪskəʊp/ *noun* an instrument which we look through to see objects which are far from us

temple /ˈtempl/ *noun* a holy building

term /tɜːm/ *noun* a part of the school year: *There are three* **terms** *in a school year.*

terrible /ˈterəbl/ *adjective* **1** causing fear: *We saw a* **terrible** *storm.* **2** very bad: *Your writing is* **terrible.** **terribly** *adverb*: *It is* **terribly** (= very) *hot.*

terrify /ˈterɪfaɪ/ *verb* (*present participle* **terrifying,** *past* **terrified**) to fill with fear: *The animals were* **terrified** *by the storm.*

throw /θrəʊ/ *verb* (*present participle* **throwing,** *past tense* **threw** /θruː/, *past participle* **thrown**) **1** to send something through the air by moving your arm: *He* **threw** *the ball to me, and I caught it.* **2** to move one's body or part of one's body suddenly: *He* **threw** *his arms up. Don't* **throw away** *your old shoes, give them to me.*

time capsule /ˈtaɪm kæpsjuːl/ *noun* a container in which you put things for a future generation to see

tin /tɪn/ *noun* **1** (*no plural*) a soft, white metal **2** a container made of this metal: *Food which has been closed up in* **tins** *is called* **tinned** *food.*

tiny /ˈtaɪnɪ/ *adjective* (**tinier, tiniest**) very small

ton /tʌn/ *noun* **1** a measure of weight equal to 2,240 pounds **2** a measure of weight equal to 1,000 kilos: *1,000 kilos is a* **metric ton.**

tongue /tʌŋ/ *noun* the part inside the mouth that moves: *Our* **tongue** *helps us to talk and to taste things.*

tour /tʊəʳ/ *noun* **1** a journey during which several places are visited: *They have gone on a* **tour.** **2** a trip to or through a place: *We went on a* **tour** *of the city.*

tournament /ˈtʊənəmənt/ *noun* a competition in which several games are played: *a chess* **tournament** / *a tennis* **tournament**

tower /ˈtaʊəʳ/ *noun* a tall narrow building or part of a building: *a church* **tower**

track /træk/ *noun* **1** a rough path **2** a special path for races

tradition /trəˈdɪʃn/ *noun* old customs or knowledge passed on from parents to their children: *It is a* **tradition** *that the young look after the old in their family.*

traffic jam /ˈtræfɪk dʒæm/ *noun* a line of cars and other vehicles which can move forward only very slowly, or not at all

treasure /ˈtreʒəʳ/ *noun* (*no plural*) a collection of gold, silver, etc.: *The* **treasure** *dug out of the earth was a box of gold coins.*

try /traɪ/ *verb* (*present participle* **trying,** *past* **tried**) **1** to do one's best to do something: *He* **tried** *to climb the tree, but he could not.* **2** to test something: *Have you* **tried** *this chocolate? She* **tried on** *the dress to see if it would fit. She* **tried out** *several cars* (= she drove them to see if she liked them) *before she chose one. I* **tried out** *a new recipe for dinner.*

turtle /ˈtɜːtl/ *noun* an animal which has a hard round shell over its body, and lives mainly in the sea

typical /ˈtɪpɪkl/ *adjective* having the usual behaviour or characteristics of a kind of person or thing: *The house is* **typical** *of the buildings of the period. It was* **typical** *of her to be late.*

U

unconscious /ʌnˈkɒnʃəs/ *adjective* not knowing what is happening or feeling anything: *After she hit her head she was* **unconscious** *for several minutes*

underground¹ /ˈʌndəgraʊnd/ *noun* a railway which goes under the ground: *to travel by* **underground**

underground² *adjective*: *an* **underground** *train*

uniform /ˈjuːnɪfɔːm/ *noun* clothes worn for a special job or for school: *The soldiers were wearing* **uniform.**

121

MINI-DICTIONARY

universe /'juːnɪvɜːs/ noun all the stars, space, etc. that we know about

upright /'ʌpraɪt/ adjective straight up and down: *Put the bottle* **upright**, *not on its side.*

upset /ʌp'set/ verb (present participle **upsetting**, past **upset**) **1** to knock over: *I* **upset** *the soup all over the table.* **2** to make unhappy or worried: *James was* **upset** *because he had lost his ticket. The news was very* **upsetting**. **3** to spoil something that was planned: *The storm* **upset** *our plans for a party outside.*

upwards /'ʌpwədz/ adverb from a lower to a higher place; towards the sky or top of anything: *The plane flew* **upwards**. *The people were all looking* **upwards**.

V

valuable /'væljuːəbəl/ adjective worth a lot: *This house is very* **valuable**; *it would cost you a lot of money.*

vampire /'væmpaɪəʳ/ noun an imaginary creature which is said to suck people's blood: *Count Dracula was a* **vampire**.

vegetarian¹ /ˌvedʒə'teɪrɪən/ noun a person who does not eat meat or fish: *I'm a* **vegetarian**.

vegetarian² adjective: *a* **vegetarian** *restaurant*

vibrate /vaɪ'breɪt/ verb (present participle **vibrating**, past **vibrated**) to shake quickly backwards and forwards: *The bus* **vibrated** *when the driver started the engine.*
vi'bration noun

view /vjuː/ noun **1** something you see: *The house has a* **view** *over the sea.* **2** an opinion: *What is your* **view** *on school punishments?*

village /'vɪlɪdʒ/ noun a small place where people live, not so large as a town

violent /'vaɪələnt/ adjective having great force: *a* **violent** *storm* **violence** noun (no plural)

W

war /wɔːʳ/ noun fighting between nations: *The two countries were* **at war** *for two years. One country* **declared war on** (= said they were going to fight) *another.*

warm /wɔːm/ verb to make or become warm: *The hot drink* **warmed** *him. He* **warmed up** *some soup for supper. I'll put the fire on – the room will soon* **warm up**.

waste¹ /weɪst/ verb (present participle **wasting**, past **wasted**) to use something wrongly or use too much of something: *Don't* **waste** *the water – there isn't much.*

waste² noun **1** an act of wasting: *It is a* **waste** *to throw away good food.* **2** used, damaged, or unwanted things: *The* **waste** *from the factory was taken away in lorries.*

water ski /'wɔːtə skiː/ verb (present participle **water skiing**, past **water skied**) to go over water wearing skis, while you are pulled along by a boat: *Let's go* **waterskiing**!

wave /weɪv/ noun one of curving lines of water on the surface of the sea which rise and fall

weapon /'wepən/ noun a thing with which we fight: *A gun is a* **weapon**.

weigh /weɪ/ verb **1** to measure how heavy a thing is: *He* **weighed** *the fish.* **2** to have a weight of: *The fish* **weighed** *two kilos.*

weight noun (no plural) the heaviness of anything: *The baby's* **weight** *was four kilos.*

weightlifting /'weɪtlɪftɪŋ/ noun (no plural) the sport of lifting heavy pieces of metal (= weights) to show how strong you are and to become stronger

werewolf /'weəwʊlf/ noun (plural **werewolves**) an imaginary person who changes into a wolf at certain times

whale /weɪl/ noun a very large animal that lives in the sea; it is not a fish but feeds its young with milk

wheel /wiːl/ noun an object made of a larger circle which turns around a smaller circle, to which it is joined: **Wheels** *make cars, lorries, and bicycles move.*

whisper /'wɪspəʳ/ verb to speak very quietly: *The two girls were whispering in the library.*

wide /waɪd/ adjective (**wider**, **widest**) large from side to side; broad

wildlife /'waɪldlaɪf/ noun (no plural) animals and plants which are living in their natural surroundings: *We started a campaign to protect the* **wildlife** *in the area.*

win /wɪn/ verb (present participle **winning**, past **won** /wʌn/) **1** to be first or do best in a competition, race, or fight: *Who* **won** *the race? I* **won** *but David came second.* **2** to be given something because one has done well in a race or competition: *He* **won** *the first prize in the competition.*
winner noun

windsurfing /'wɪndsɜːfɪŋ/ noun (no plural) the sport of riding along on the sea on a long narrow board with a sail

wise /waɪz/ adjective (**wiser**, **wisest**) having or showing good sense and cleverness: **wise** *advice* **wisdom** noun

wizard /'wɪzəd/ noun a man who is believed to have magic powers

wolf /wʊlf/ noun (plural **wolves**) a wild animal of the dog family, which usually lives in forests

wonder¹ /'wʌndəʳ/ verb **1** to express a wish to know: *I* **wonder** *why James is always late for school.* **2** to be surprised: *We all* **wondered** *at his rudeness.*

wonder² noun **1** (no plural) a feeling of surprise and admiration: *They were filled with* **wonder** *when they saw the spaceship.* **No wonder** (= it is no surprise) *he is not hungry; he has been eating sweets all day.* **2** something or someone causing this feeling **wonderful** adjective unusually good: **wonderful** *news*

work out /ˈwɜːk aʊt/ verb **1** to find the solution to: *She* **worked out** *the answer to the problem.* **2** to exercise your body to make it strong and slim: *He* **works out** *every week at the gym.*

worry /'wʌri/ verb (present participle **worrying**, past **worried**) to feel or make someone feel anxious: *My parents* **wprry** *(about me) if I come home late. The news of the fighting* **worried** *us.*

Y

yourself /jə'self/ (plural **yourselves** /jə'selvz/) **1** the same person as the one that the speaker is talking to: *Look at* **yourself** *in the mirror. You can't lift that* **by yourself** (= without help). *Why are you playing* **by yourself** (= alone)? **2** (used to make **you** have a stronger meaning): *You told me the story* **yourself**.

Z

zero-gravity /'zɪərəʊ 'grævɪti/ noun (no plural) the absence of gravity

zodiac /'zəʊdɪæk/ noun a diagram showing the position of the planets and stars at different times, which is used to see how the planets and stars may influence your character and life: *What sign of the* **zodiac** *are you? I'm Scorpio.*

Fact or fantasy?

Lesson 15 – Fact
Lesson 17 – Fact
Lesson 20 – Fantasy